VOLUME I
THE ORIGINAL WAY

RESTORING
THE GLORY

THE ANCIENT PATHS
REDISCOVERED

AUTHOR OF *THE HEALING POWER OF THE ROOTS*
DOMINIQUAE BIERMAN

ZIONS GOSPEL
PRESS

Restoring the Glory: Volume I © 2020 by Dominiquae Bierman

All rights reserved. This book may not be copied or reprinted for commercial gain or profit. The use of short quotations or occasional page copying for personal or group study is permitted and encouraged. Permission will be granted upon request.

First paperback edition: September 2019
Second paperback edition: December 2020

Unless otherwise identified, all scripture quotations are from the *Tree of Life Version* (TLV) and the *New American Standard Bible* (NASB).

Tree of Life Version. © 2015 by the *Messianic Jewish Family Bible Society*. Used by permission of the *Messianic Jewish Family Bible Society*. New American Standard Bible. © 1995 by the *Lockman Foundation*. Used by permission, all rights reserved.

Words such as Jesus, Christ, Lord, and God have been changed by the author, back to their original Hebrew renderings, Yeshua, Yahveh, and Elohim.

Paperback ISBN: 978-1-953502-23-0
E-Book ISBN: 978-1-953502-24-7

Published by *Zion's Gospel Press*
shalom@zionsgospel.com | 52 Tuscan Way, Ste 202-412,
St. Augustine Florida, 32092, USA

First Printing September 2019, Second Printing December 2020

Printed in the United States of America

To the ashes of my people in Auschwitz.
For the sin of silence, for the sin of indifference;
for the sin of secret complicity of the neutral;
for the closing of borders; for the washing of hands;
for all that was done; for all not done.

OTHER BOOKS BY ARCHBISHOP DR. DOMINIQUAE BIERMAN

Order now online: www.kad-esh.org/shop/

The MAP Revolution (Free E-Book)
Find Out Why Revival Does not Come... Yet!

The Identity Theft
The Return of the 1st Century Messiah

The Healing Power of the Roots
It's a Matter of Life or Death!

Grafted In
Discover How to Return to the Former Glory

Sheep Nations
It's Time to Take the Nations!

Stormy Weather
Judgment Has Already Begun, Revival is Knocking at the Door

Yeshua is the Name
The Important Restoration of the Original Hebrew Name of the Messiah

The Bible Cure for Africa and the Nations
The Key to the Restoration of All Africa

The Key of Abraham
The Blessing... or the Curse?

Yes!
The Dramatic Salvation of Archbishop Dr. Dominiquae Bierman

Eradicating the Cancer of Religion
Hint: All People Have It

Restoration of the Holy Giving
Releasing the True 1,000 Fold Blessing

Vision Negev
The Awesome Restoration of the Sephardic Jews

Defeating Depression
This Book is a Kiss from Heaven

From Sickology to a Healthy Logic
The Product of 18 Years Walking Through Psychiatric Hospitals

ATG: Addicts Turning to God
The Biblical Way to Handle Addicts and Addictions

The Woman Factor by Rabbi Baruch Bierman
Freedom From Womanphobia

The Revival of the Third Day
(Free E-Book)
The Return to Yeshua the Jewish Messiah

The Identity Theft
The Return of the 1st Century Messiah

ALSO AVAILABLE
MUSIC ALBUMS
www.kad-esh.org/shop/

The Key of Abraham
Abba Shebashamayim
Uru
Retorno

GRM ISRAELI BIBLE SCHOOL
www.grmbibleschool.com
For more information or to order, please contact us:
info@kad-esh.org
Phone: +1 (972) 301-7087
www.kad-esh.org
www.unitednationsforisrael.org

AN EARLY MESSIANIC SYMBOL

This sign has been found in pottery and on walls of what is believed to be the meeting rooms of second-Century believers in Jerusalem. During an archaeological excavation in recent years, repeatedly found is this symbol (with variations).

Experts feel this symbol was a sign of unity between the Jewish believers and their Christian brethren in the rest of the Roman Empire. Some suggest that it was also a secret symbol of identification in times of persecution.

CONTENTS

It's Time to Return the Glory!.................. 1
Two Weddings and One Divorce................ 5

Part A. Restoration............................17
Chapter 1. Thirsty for Living Waters?............. 19
Chapter 2. The Roots of Our Belief System........ 29
Chapter 3. The Return of the Holy Spirit.......... 35
Chapter 4. Draining the Swamp of Religion....... 49
Chapter 5. Restoring the Gospel Made in Zion ... 57
Chapter 6. The Second Exodus..................... 69
Chapter 7. The Third Day Revival 75
Chapter 8. The Rule of Messiah on Earth 95
Chapter 9. The Trick... or the Tree?............... 105
Chapter 10. Christmas in Sukkot?.................. 127
Chapter 11. Hanukkah Time........................ 135
Chapter 12. The Hanukkah Turning Point 141

Part B. Truth and Lies 147
Chapter 13. Blowing the Dust Off the Truth..... 149
Chapter 14. Common Deadly Deceptions 177

Chapter 15. Flee the Kabbalah Deception 195
Chapter 16. Removing False Assumptions 207
Chapter 17. Dispelling Superstitions and Myths . 215
Chapter 18. The Noahide Lie 227

Part C. Teachings 235
Chapter 19. Grooming Your Spirit.................. 237
Chapter 20. Removing the Leaven of Unbelief..... 245
Chapter 21. Religion vs. Reality.................... 259
Chapter 22. Is There a Cure for Religion? 269
Chapter 23. The Effects of Religion................ 277
Chapter 24. Wounded by Religion 287
Chapter 25. The Kingdoms of this World.......... 293
Chapter 26. Bold as a Lion 301
Chapter 27. My Queen Esther...................... 313
Appendix I. Get Equipped & Partner with Us...... 325
Appendix II. Bibliography 327

VOLUME I
THE ORIGINAL WAY

RESTORING THE GLORY

INTRODUCTION
IT'S TIME TO RETURN THE GLORY!

> Thus says the Lord, "Stand by the ways and see and ask for the ancient paths, where the good way is, and walk in it; and you will find rest for your souls. But they said, 'We will not walk in it.'
>
> — *Jeremiah 6:16*

A THOUSAND HUMAN EXPLANATIONS will not be able to define the glory of YHVH. No books will manage to do His glory service.

My hopes and prayers are that by restoring the understanding of the Gospel and the Word from the eyes of the First Century Church, we will be able to become recipients of His glory.

The word for "glory" in Hebrew is *kavod*. It is rooted in the word *kaved*, which means "heavy, weighty, honor and respect." When His glory fills His House, the gates and foundations shake.

> One called out to another and said: "Holy, holy, holy, is A‌donai-Tzva'ot! The whole earth is full of His glory." Then the posts of the door trembled at the voice of those who called, and the House was filled with smoke. Then I said: "Oy to me! For I am ruined! For I am a man of unclean lips, and I am dwelling among a people of unclean lips. For my eyes have seen the King, A‌donai-Tzva'ot!"
>
> — Isaiah 6:3-5 TLV

One day His Spirit whispered into my heart, saying, "I cannot pour out my glory, as many are asking me to do. My glory is too heavy for the present-day foundation of My House. First, restore the original Hebrew foundation, then I can pour out My glory. As it is, My glory would destroy the Church for the foundation is faulty."

This book is a compilation of a few of my weekly Shabbat letters. They will give you a taste of the original foundation of the First Century disciples who were Jewish. Some chapters will expose everyday deceptions believed by most to be true.

As you read with an open, humble heart, may the Spirit of Revelation open your eyes to the original foundation of what I call, "the Gospel made in Zion."

I pray that your eyes will open, and you proceed to implement His Truth as revealed to you in this book's pages. Then you will start the journey of awakening, revival, and the restoration of His glory.

For the earth will be filled with knowing the glory of A‍DONAI, as the waters cover the sea.

— Habakkuk 2:14 TLV

For His kavod;
Archbishop Dr. Dominiquae Bierman
President of *Kad-Esh MAP Ministries* and *The United Nations for Israel*

PREFACE
TWO WEDDINGS AND ONE DIVORCE

> But if some of the branches were broken off, and you, being a wild olive, were grafted in among them and became partaker with them of the rich root of the olive tree, do not be arrogant toward the branches; but if you are arrogant, remember that it is not you who supports the root, but the root supports you.
>
> — *Romans 11:17-18*

THE FIRST AND original Church was married to a Jewish Husband by the name of Yeshua the Messiah and into His family, the Jewish people. (See Ephesians 2:14 and Romans 11.) The Wedding Ceremony took place in Jerusalem. It was ratified and sealed by the spilling of the Blood of the Husband and by the breaking of His Body. (See Luke 22:15–20.) The time of this marriage was the Holy Biblical Feast of Passover. The fruit of this awesome wedding was thousands and thousands of people, both Jews and Gentiles saved and healed. Even the shadow of this holy bride healed the sick, as signs and wonders and miracles followed her wherever she went in the name of her Husband Yeshua.

This marriage led the wife into much suffering. Many in the world did not love her Husband and tried to kill her by persecuting her and even throwing her to the lions during the Roman Empire's reign of terror. Those were hard years. After many years of suffering, Yeshua's wife had become weary. He had gone to prepare a place for her and had not come back yet. She started to get tired of her lifestyle as an outcast, persecuted, and hunted at every corner. She longed for peace at any price.

She longed for the warm embrace of a Husband who would provide her with peace and security here on this earth. At her weakest point, an earthly king appeared. (See Matthew 10:34, John 14:27, Jeremiah 8:11.)

This earthly king was influential and powerful by worldly standards. He could stop the killing and persecution against her. He could give her the security she longed for: If only she would agree to divorce this Jewish Husband of hers and utterly separate from His family Israel, and from that Book that she treasured so much – where He had left her all of His instructions and the family legacy of God's Word.

This powerful king seemed to be a spiritual man. He claimed that her Jewish Husband had appeared to him in a dream and had given him the crown of the Roman Empire. His deceptive charm and appealing manners managed to attract the very weary Bride of Messiah, but not all were deceived. There was a portion of the Bride/Church/Ecclesia that was not fooled by the charms of this deceitful king. These were the Messianic Jews of the time.

They were too rooted in the writings of the Holy Book and the Ancient Hebrew Scriptures to be deceived. But the vast majority of the believers at that time were Gentiles, and they did not want any more suffering on behalf of The Book, its Author, or His Family.

They wanted freedom and peace at all cost.

The powerful Constantine sang the song of peace and safety and prepared a bed of roses. The Gentile portion of the Church slept with him, falling into violent adultery and wounding the heart of her heavenly Jewish Husband. To appease the conscience of this adulterous church, Constantine decided to legalize this unholy union in the year 325 A.D. through a wedding ceremony called the Council of Nicaea and drawing up an ungodly and illegal marriage contract called the *Nicene Creed*.

He used his worldly power to draw all the Gentile church fathers, which for the most part were already anti-Semitic and hated their Jewish roots. These church fathers were to be witnesses of this horrendous divorce and the adulterous new marriage between the predominantly Gentile Church and another Jesus, a product of Constantine's creation.

This alternative Savior came with another family, another book (totally disconnected from the Ancient Hebrew Writings), other customs, laws, festivals, traditions, and ways of measuring time.

Knowing that his brand-new wife was *accustomed* to worshiping God, he organized for her a god that would suit her perfectly by not demanding any holiness from her. He presented a god of peace that was lenient towards a mixture of paganism and holiness: An all-inclusive god, who accepted all traditions and blended them into one.

Now Passover and First Fruits, which was the festival of Yeshua's Resurrection, would become The Feast of Ishtar, the goddess of fertility, or Easter with bunny rabbits and Easter eggs. (At that time eggs were dipped in the blood of the babies sacrificed to the goddess, thus the tradition of painting the eggs.)

Now the Day of Worship would change from Shabbat to Sunday to eternalize the sun god who for now would be called Jesus – yet it was another Jesus and certainly not Yeshua, the Jewish Messiah.

Then the day of the Winter Solstice of witchcraft, called *Saturnalia* or *Paganalia,* celebrated on the 25th of December in the Roman Empire, was to acquire the name Christmas and would *celebrate* the birth of this false Messiah. For the true Messiah was born during the Holy Biblical Feast of Tabernacles and followed the Hebrew Biblical Calendar, not the Roman one. (See Daniel 7:25-27, Jeremiah 10:2-4 about the Christmas tree.)

The Ancient Holy Book of the Hebrew Scriptures was to become obsolete, and its laws were done away. Instead, Constantine compiled the Apostolic Writings, the letters of Paul and others into a new holy book and called it the New Testament. He gave this holy book his own *perverse* interpretation, completely divorced from the foundational

Hebrew Writings whom he and his followers called the "Old Testament" (Matthew 5:17-21).

In rejecting their custom, we may transmit to our descendants the legitimate way of celebrating Easter...We ought not therefore to have anything in common with the Jew, for the Savior has shown us another way; our worship following a more legitimate and more convenient course (the order of the days of the week); And consequently, in unanimously adopting this mode, we desire dearest brethren to separate ourselves from the detestable company of the Jew. (Excerpt from *The Nicene Creed,* year 325, found in *Eusebius, Vita Const. Lib III 18-20*)

This creed and its instructions are still followed by most Christians today with the celebration of Easter, Christmas, Sunday (replacing *Shabbat*), and the rejection of the Laws of God.

Indeed, a new religion had been born. It had a Gentile god by the name of Jesus Christ; an apostle by the name of Constantine; a new book by the name of the New Testament (although compiled from the Apostolic Writings, which are *completely* Yah inspired, it was deceitfully *interpreted* through gentile eyes and gentile theologians); new traditions, and unholy festivals such as Easter, Christmas, Sunday, and Halloween.

Most importantly... *No Jews...* No, not even the Messiah.

WHAT HAS BEEN THE FRUIT OF THIS ADULTEROUS MARRIAGE?

"Either make the tree good and its fruit good, or else make the tree bad and its fruit bad; for a tree is known by its fruit."
— Matthew 12:33

The fruit of the first holy matrimony were salvations and healings.

The fruit of this ungodly and *pagan* marriage was forced conversions and *murder,* yes, even mass destructions of the family of Yeshua the Messiah, (the true Husband), in the name of the false Jesus Christ god created by Constantine.

A god who, according to Constantine in the Nicene Creed, had shown us another way. What was that way? It is a way of jealousy, hatred, killing, destruction, and *lawlessness.* Horrendous Christian events such as pogroms, the Holy Inquisition, and the Holocaust, have taken place since this ungodly 4th-Century marriage and the creation of this false religion.

The hatred conveyed in the Nicene Creed against the Jews and anything Jewish, including the Torah and the Old Testament, has continued through the great Protestant Reformation of the 16th Century, and it still influences Christians today.

The following excerpt is from *Our Hands are Stained with Blood* by Michael Brown, as he quotes directly from Martin Luther's writings. Luther wrote this after he was frustrated from trying to evangelize the Jews and when he was old and sick:

> What shall we Christians do with this damned rejected race of Jews? First, their synagogues should be set on

fire. Secondly, their homes should likewise be broken down and destroyed. Thirdly, they should be deprived of their prayer books and Talmuds. Fourthly, their rabbis must be forbidden under threat of death to teach anymore. Fifthly, passports and traveling privileges should be absolutely forbidden to the Jews...To sum up dear princes and nobles, who have Jews in your domains, if this advice of mine does not suit you, then find a better one. So that you and we may all be free of this insufferable, devilish burden – the Jews.

Hitler followed Luther's instructions meticulously and quoted him while doing so. The fruit? Over six million Jews exterminated in horrendous death camps and gas chambers, and many survivors scarred for life.

A PROPHETIC ALTAR CALL

> "After two days He will revive us; on the third day He will raise us up, that we may live in His sight. Let us know; let us pursue the knowledge of Yahveh. His going forth is established as the morning; He will come to us like the rain, like the latter and former rain to the earth."
>
> — Hosea 6:2-3

The Third Day is upon us, the Third Millennium, and this is the Father's call to His Third Day Church:

Come, let us return to Yeshua, to our Jewish Messiah, His Jewish Family and His ancient Hebrew Scriptures. Come, let us reinterpret the New Testament through the eyes of the Holy Scriptures. Let us separate ourselves from our pagan husband,

Constantine, and his false Jesus and let us go back to the *True Messiah Yeshua*, to His Father's Laws and Precepts, to *true* divine holy Grace, to *true* love and holiness. Let us return to Jerusalem, and let us be made whole from centuries of adultery and paganism, as we go back to the original Apostolic Jewish roots of our faith.

In Yeshua's love and brokenness;
Archbishop Dr. Dominiquae and Rabbi Baruch Bierman
Founders of *Kad-Esh MAP Ministries & The United Nations for Israel*

DISCLAIMER
What this book is not saying:

1. *It is not* saying to go back to the laws of Rabbinic Judaism.
2. *It is not* implying that all Christians have anti-Semitism.
3. *It is not* disqualifying the countless believers who call on the name of Jesus Christ meaning the true Jewish Messiah Yeshua.
4. *It is not* disqualifying worshiping on Sunday, Monday, Tuesday or any other day.
5. *It is not* disqualifying the New Testament as Bible (only the wrong, "divorced" interpretations of it).

VOCABULARY

Before you begin to read this book, I would like you to be familiar with some renewed terminology that will help your understanding. In any new move of God, there is new, or renewed terminology introduced. It is no different in the case of this End-time move of restoration. Here are four terms which are used throughout the entire book. I would like you to be familiar with:

1. Yahveh

Yahveh is the name of the LORD as revealed to Moses and used throughout the Prophetic Writings. *Yahveh* means the "I AM" and the "Ever-Present God."

This name is often used in conjunction with the name; ELOHIM, which is the name of the "Creator God."

2. Yahveh ELOHIM

In Hebrew, *Yahveh ELOHIM* translates to "The I AM who is the Creator." The short way of saying Yahveh is *Yah* as in "Halelu-Yah." So, many times I will use the word Yah instead of "God."

3. ADONAI

ADONAI is the Hebrew word for "master" or "lord."

4. The Torah

Torah is the Hebrew word for "Instruction in Righteousness," commonly called law.

In this book, Torah only refers to the Law of Yahveh in the Five Books of Moses and Law throughout the Bible. In this book, the Torah does not apply to rabbinical laws or man-made traditions. In a place where I mention a rabbinical tradition, I will refer to it as such.

The Torah includes three types of charges:

- Commandments
- Statutes or Judgments
- Laws or Precepts

> **Because that Abraham obeyed My voice, and kept My charge, My commandments, My statutes, and My laws.**
> **— Genesis 26:5**

Notice that before Moses was given the Torah at Mount Sinai, Abraham *already* walked and obeyed the Torah. Abraham already followed the Torah since the Torah of the Living Yah (God) is eternal.

- The Commandments are eternal (referring to the Ten Commandments).
- The Statutes are also eternal and connected with holiness and worship. Note: Following the Statutes connected with Temple Worship requires more background knowledge. Since we are now the Temple of the Holy Spirit, an interpretation from the Holy Spirit is needed about how to follow them today.
- The Precepts are eternal principles, though the actual instructions were temporary and only relevant to the issues of the times they were given. So, today, we keep the principles and apply them

to our times. As we walk with the Holy Spirit of Yah, He continues to give us precepts daily!

Here is the ticket to lifelong success and prosperity:

This Book of the Law (Torah) shall not depart from your mouth, but you shall meditate in it day and night, that you may observe to do according to all that is written in it. For then you will make your way prosperous, and then you will have good success.

— Joshua 1:8

Abraham, who is the father of the faith, understood and walked in the way which he had been given. Also in these End-times, the Torah is being restored: A revelation by the Holy Spirit to the Church. As we meditate in Yah's Holy Commandments, Judgments and Precepts; the Word will become flesh in us and will produce the fruit of obedience. This obedience will make us blessed, successful, and prosperous.

5. Yeshua

Yeshua (commonly called Jesus Christ) is the real Hebrew name for the Jewish Messiah. In Hebrew, Yeshua means "Salvation, deliverance, and redemption." Throughout this book, I will use His Hebrew name only.

Yeshua is the Torah made flesh or the Living Torah. As you follow Him, and His *Ruach HaKodesh* (Holy Spirit) He will lead you to the Truth.

And you shall know the truth, and the truth shall make you *free*.

— John 8:32

PART A
RESTORATION

CHAPTER 1

THIRSTY FOR LIVING WATERS?

The Spirit and the bride says, "Come!" And let the one who hears say, "Come!" Let the one who is thirsty come; and let the one who wishes take the free gift of the water of life.

— *Revelation 22:17*

We have recently ministered in Papua New Guinea (PNG) where a true End-time awakening of a nation is happening. This awakening is impacting all parts of the society, from the smallest to the greatest. But how did it start? And what is the *key*? I have always said that the power is in the *small* and the Word says that as well.

For who has despised the day of small things?

— *Zechariah 4:10*

Everything meaningful starts small and looks insignificant. That was the case in the Elijah revival of righteousness in Northern Israel over 2,700 years ago:

> It came about at the seventh time, that he said, "Behold, a cloud as small as a man's hand is coming up from the sea." And he said, "Go up, say to Ahab, 'Prepare your chariot and go down, so that the heavy shower does not stop you.
>
> — 1 Kings 18:44

That was enough for the great Prophet *Elyahu* (Elijah) to tell the wicked King Ahab to run back home because an abundance of rain was coming! However, in the natural, it was only a small insignificant cloud.

REVIVAL CAME BECAUSE I MET ONE PAPUA NEW GUINEAN

> For as through the one man's disobedience the many were made sinners, even so through the obedience of the One the many will be made righteous.
>
> — Romans 5:19

In the year 2000, during the high holidays, I met one intercessor from PNG that came to *Yerushalayim* (Jerusalem) to pray. He heard my name and asked: "Are you Dominiquae Bierman, the writer of *The Healing Power of the Roots*?"

"Yes I am," I said.

"I am from Papua New Guinea and I have read your book, and it has impacted my life!" he replied.

I was amazed! I had never been to PNG, how did my book get there? Most surely heavenly couriers! (This has happened a lot with this particular book. It has traversed the world in many languages without an official distribution.)

Has this precious intercessor been praying for us to go to PNG? Has he been praying for us to administer this life and death message to his country, which claims to be 97% Christian, yet remains full of tribal idolatry? I do not know. I do not remember his name, and I never saw him again. This meeting was a seemingly small and unimportant occurrence! However, exactly seven years later a lady knocked at the door of our home and Ministry in *Mevasseret,* Zion in the Mountains of Jerusalem.

"My name is Elizabeth, I am from Papua New Guinea," she explained. "And I have come to find the Jewish Parents of my nation."

She came bearing a gift, an offering, a check drawn from the Bank of PNG. I was amazed and asked her, "Do you know who we are, have you read any of my books?"

"No," she responded, "But the Holy Spirit directed me to you."

The rest is "His-story"!

When Elizabeth arrived, we were packing ourselves and the ministry, as YHVH was relocating us to Eilat. Elizabeth, (now Apostle-Pastor Elizabeth George) remained with us as we packed.

Slowly, but surely, other Papua New Guineans started to frequent our Sukkot tours and our Eilat Prayer Tower. They always arrived bestowing honor and bearing gifts, just like the Three Wise Men from the East at the birth of Messiah. They were being guided, propelled by something more significant than all of us, by the Holy Spirit, the Ruach HaKodesh of

YHVH. They were *thirsty* for Living Waters, and they were willing to pay the price for it although it was being offered to them *freely*.

FREE WATERS WITH A HIGH PRICE TAG

Large crowds were traveling with Yeshua, and turning to them he said: "If anyone comes to me and does not hate father and mother, wife and children, brothers and sisters—yes, even their own life—such a person cannot be my disciple. And whoever does not carry their cross and follow me cannot be my disciple. Suppose one of you wants to build a tower. Won't you first sit down and estimate the cost to see if you have enough money to complete it? For if you lay the foundation and are not able to finish it, everyone who sees it will ridicule you, saying, 'This person began to build and wasn't able to finish.'"

— Luke 14:25-30

As the PNG pilgrimages to our Eilat Prayer Tower and Sukkot Tours continued to increase, Pastor Elizabeth introduced me to Pastors Charlie and Mollie George. They, in turn, began to be used more and more in orchestrating my first visit to PNG in 2014, and our recent visit in 2017 and 2019. The MAP (Messianic Apostolic Prophetic) Movement in PNG began to grow. Our first disciples in PNG, Pastor Elizabeth George, Pastors Mollie and Charlie George, and Pastor Brian N'dreland, graduated from our GRM Bible School. But what can four pastors do? The same as *one* intercessor who came to pray and *one* obedient prophetess who began looking for the Jewish parents of PNG!

Everything *big* starts *small* because someone is thirsty enough for the Waters of Life that are given *freely*, and yet, it demands "the counting of the cost." Revivals are *free*, but it requires that we lay our lives, our finances and our time on the Altar of YHVH: On the altar of truth and revival!

GREAT HONOR

> I will bless those who bless you, and whoever curses you I will curse; and all peoples on earth will be blessed through you.
> – Genesis 12:3

It is still happening. YHVH is still blessing *all* the families of the earth through the people of Israel—whoever honors us will be blessed. The Church at large dishonored the Jews for centuries, and it brought death, but as peoples and nations turn to *honor* us, it will bring great blessings. YHVH promised this, and His Word is established in heaven no matter how much the devil and his followers hate it! We are to be a blessing to the Nations and honoring us as Israelis, as Jews that bring the Gospel, the Living Torah, Yeshua to the Nations, *releases* the blessing and *revival*:

> For if their (the Jews) rejection brought reconciliation to the world, what will their (the Jews) acceptance be but life from the dead?
> – Romans 11:15

What triggers a glorious response from the Holy Spirit? I can trace it to great honor: Every Papua New Guinean that arrived in Israel to visit us seriously honored us and Israel and came bearing gifts! They came as Cornelius, and YHVH is answering and visiting them just like He did Cornelius who attracted His divine attention by *praying* and *giving* alms to the Jews.

> **Now there was a man at Caesarea named Cornelius, a centurion of what was called the Italian cohort, a devout man and one who feared God with all his household, and gave many alms to the Jewish people and prayed to God continually.**
> **— Acts 10:1-2**

The honor Cornelius gave opened the door for the Gentiles to be saved. In the same way, the door has been opened for PNG to be saved and to become a Sheep Nation! From *one* intercessor who, in the year 2000, came to *Yerushalayim* to pray, and *one* prophetess who, seven years later, knocked on our door bearing gifts, thousands have been drinking of the Waters of Life freely. Those who have been liberally drinking have included those in the prisons, in the government, in the great cities, in the highlands and the villages! Our precious pastors have taken the Waters of Life freely, at a high cost, to the remotest parts of the highlands and the surrounding islands. These faithful servants of God make copies of our Shabbat Letters and hand-carry them to places that are not reached by the internet! People in Papua New Guinea are *thirsty* for the Living Waters of the Torah, the Spirit, for Yeshua the Jewish Messiah, for the Gospel made in Zion.

THIRSTY ENOUGH TO PAY THE PRICE

What a dichotomy—free waters and yet you have to *pay the price*. How can that be? But that is the mystery of the Kingdom: Truth is *free*, yet it needs to be *purchased*:

> **Buy the truth and sell it not!**
>
> — Proverbs 23:23

Many arrived at our meetings in PNG after walking for *many* days and in all kinds of weather. In some areas, there are no roads, and a plane ticket is too expensive for most. Their *thirst* drove them to *walk*, to pay the price to come! A thirsty person is willing to do *anything* to get to *water*.

Just ask those who live in remote villages in Africa where there is no running water, and they will tell you how people walk up to 20 miles to get to a well, and then return carrying the heavy load of the precious liquid called *water*. It is the same in the spirit: The thirsty ones will be willing to walk for days for a drink of the true Living Waters. And we could see them worshiping and praising with such passion as we served them the Living Waters, the Living Torah, the Living Messiah – the Gospel made in Zion! They drank with *gusto*!

> **Blessed are those who hunger and thirst for righteousness, for they shall be satisfied.**
>
> — Matthew 5:6

Revival does not happen until people are *thirsty* enough to pay the price for it, to pay the price to *shma*, which means "to listen and obey the word of truth." Many people want a "touch from the Spirit," but revival is not a "touch from the Spirit."

Revival happens when we allow the Cross to penetrate our hearts and souls, to convict us of sin and lead us to *Teshuva*—which means "repentance"—for the purpose of restoration!

Most people prefer Coca Cola to fresh Living Waters. They want something that will satisfy their *lust*, but it is not real *thirst*. When you are really *thirsty* only water will do—the pure Gospel made in Zion, the Living Torah!

> So that He might sanctify her, having cleansed her by the washing of water with the word, that He might present to Himself the church in all her glory, having no spot or wrinkle or any such thing; but that she would be holy and blameless.
> — Ephesians 5:26-27

NOTHING WILL DETER THE THIRSTY FROM DRINKING LIVING WATERS

> Oh, that You would rend the heavens and come down, that the mountains might quake at Your presence—as fire kindles the brushwood, as fire causes water to boil—to make Your name known to Your adversaries, that the nations may tremble at Your presence! When You did awesome things which we did not expect, You came down, the mountains quaked at Your presence. For from days of old they have not heard or perceived by ear, nor has the eye seen a God besides You, who acts in behalf of the one who waits for Him.
> — Isaiah 64:1-4

Thousands stood outside of the packed meeting hall in the City of *Lae*. There were as many outside as inside! And though this was *not* the rainy season, as I was preaching, a great rain was poured out from heaven and pounded on the roof. It sounded like thousands of horses galloping over our heads. One accompanying pastor said, "It never rains here at this time: This rain is a sign of *revival*!" As it down poured, the thousands of people *outside* the meeting hall, including their children, were getting drenched. You would have expected them to run away from the meeting to seek shelter and a dry place somewhere, but *no* – none of them left! They stayed listening to the Word from Zion followed with signs, wonders, and miracles. They kept on *drinking* the Living Waters even when the rain from heaven was drenching them. That is the *key* to a *true* revival to continue: Even when the Holy Spirit is poured out in *buckets*, keep on *drinking* of the Word, of His Torah and instructions in righteousness—allow *nothing* to deter you from *drinking* His Word!

Wherever, in whatever country, where people are *thirsty* for the *truth* of the Word, the Living Torah, and will honor Yah and His vessels sent from Zion, they will experience the outpouring of the Waters of Life freely!

> **Thus says YHVH Zevaot, "In those days ten men from all the nations will grasp the (hem of the) garment of a Jew, saying, 'Let us go with you, for we have heard that YHVH-God is with you.'"**
> **— Zechariah 8:23**

Are *you thirsty* for Living Waters?

CHAPTER 2

THE ROOTS OF OUR BELIEF SYSTEM

> "Look at the heavens and see; and behold the clouds,
> they are higher than you."
>
> — *Job 35:5*

---

*I*N ONE OF our many journeys to Auschwitz in past years we lodged in *Krakow*, Poland with the group I was teaching about the roots of the Shoah (Holocaust) and what allowed such a catastrophic event to happen.

I took my group to see the memorial of the Jews who were transported on the train to the nearby death camp of Auschwitz-Birkenau. Upon arrival at the moving memorial, I saw it had been defaced with swastikas and "death to the Jews." Three teenage girls were standing with their bicycles and smoking. When they saw us arriving they started to mock us and speak evil about the Jews while puffing smoke from their cigarettes.

I turned sharply around and eyeballed one of them saying, "the Savior that you worship as a Catholic, Jesus Christ, is a Jew so when you mock and hate the Jews, it is Him you are mocking, hating and hurting."

One of the girls who was about 16 years old dropped her cigarette and stood in attention startled and scared by my directness.

"Let me ask you all a question," I proceeded, "do you know *any* Jews? Have you ever met even one?" There are almost no Jews left in Poland since the Nazi extermination, so naturally, they all said, "No, we do not know any."

"So why do you hate and mock the Jews if you have never met even one?"

We introduced ourselves as Jews and took the girls with us to visit the ancient synagogue in *Krakow*, and this led to our praying for them under the *tallit* to break all that demonic hatred. We hugged and embraced them – they all accepted Yeshua, and one received the Holy Spirit.

So why do we believe what we believe? Why did these girls believe Jews to be evil and sub-human if they had never even met a Jew before they met us? How can people be so categoric about what they deem to be right without any research or proof? What causes you and I to be so set in our way of thinking that we are not willing to dig deeper to find out if what we believe is rooted in the truth?

> **Hear, you deaf! And look, you blind, that you may see.**
>
> — Isaiah 42:18

Words matter: Theologies and philosophies have the power to shape our belief system. Whatever "word" is spoken to us from the start will create our concept of life, our purpose, our world and our belief system. By digging into the word that shaped our lives we will find the roots of our belief system that has directed the course of our lives. That is why it is vital to train a child in the way he should go so that later he will not depart from it.

The *words* spoken into our early lives, even as far back as when we were babies in the womb, shaped our lives and the way we believe.

> **I have come as Light into the world, so that everyone who believes in Me will not remain in darkness.**
>
> — John 12:46

The LGBTQ agenda to "educate" our children that sexual deviations and perversions contrary to the way the Creator made us is acceptable, and even encouraged, is now defining a whole generation where sexual perversion, deviation, and rebellion against the Creator is the norm.

Growing up with the word of Darwinism and the survival of the species would have created a godless and ruthless generation that has no Creator to which to be accountable.

Growing up in Christianity with Replacement Theology would have created believers who despised the Jews and everything Jewish. These would be very different from the

Jewish believers in the First Century. That is why every denomination of Christianity believes itself to be the one with the Truth. They have been shaped through man-made theologies, but are they right?

We have all been taught a certain way, a particular line of thought, but is it true? To be able to humble our hearts to question if our belief system is rooted in truth is the mandate of the hour for this restless generation.

Do not be wise in your own eyes; fear the Lord and turn away from evil.
— Proverbs 3:7

Questioning and discovering the truth about our belief system will open us up for change and transformation by the One who said about Himself,

I am the Way, the Truth and the Life, no one comes to the Father but through Me.
— John 14:6

Jews, Christian's, Muslims, Atheists, Gnostic's, Hindus, Buddhists, Free Masons, and all religions and "non-religion" religions are called to question and to dig deeper into their belief system to see if it is rooted in fables, legends, man-made stories, cultural traditions, or in truth.

Palestinians are called to question what kind of belief system they are instilling into their babies, who they want to grow up to become murderers of Jews. Israelis teach their babies to love and respect *life* while Palestinians, in their schools, are teaching their kids the "culture of death and hatred."

The United Nations for Israel* is seeking to reeducate this generation regarding what the truth is about Israel, the God of Israel and the Jewish Messiah. We invite you to question and to dig deeper with the help of our books and our Israeli Bible School, GRM**, which can be attended through many different formats.

To know the truth and to make it known will bring the freedom each one of us, and this world so desperately needs.

* www.unitednationsforisrael.org
** www.grmbibleschool.com

CHAPTER 3

THE RETURN OF THE HOLY SPIRIT

> When the Day of Shavuot (Pentecost) had fully come, they were all with one accord in one place. And suddenly there came a sound from heaven, as of a rushing mighty wind, and it filled the whole house where they were sitting. Then there appeared to them divided tongues, as of fire, and one sat upon each of them. And they were all filled with the Holy Spirit and began to speak with other tongues, as the Spirit gave them utterance.
>
> — *Acts 2:1-4*

---

*T*HE OTHER DAY, I was watching a series on T.V. about some practices in the Catholic Church in the late 1600s and it was horrendous! I saw the self-flagellation, and the self-abasement as priests and nuns inflicted pain and blood-gushing wounds upon themselves to "subdue the lusts of the flesh." When they were bleeding profusely from gaping wounds of self-inflicted punishment, they would enter into a supposed "Holy Spirit frenzy." They would lift their hands in complete and raptured devotion and scream words like "now I can feel you," "I can feel your presence," etc. It looked like a Pentecostal Meeting except for the blood gushing from their open wounds. I was appalled at that depth of deception that leads to demonic activity. This practice was not a blessed activity of the Holy Spirit! My spirit was so grieved inside of me. So many want Him and only find *religion*.

It reminded me of the Muslims. They do the same things during their feast called the Day of Ashura. It happens on the tenth day of the Islamic month of *Muharram*, and *Ashura* has been observed on this day annually for 1,300 years. Both adults and children inflict punishment upon themselves and make cuts in their bodies until blood gushes out from their heads and bodies to please the demon-god Allah!

This practice is exactly what happened at the time of *Elyahu* (Elijah) the Prophet when he contested the idolatrous religious systems of his time. The people on Mount Carmel where trying to entreat Baal to answer them by inflicting punishment upon themselves and cutting themselves with sharp instruments until they bled!

> **It came about at noon, that Elijah mocked them and said, "Call out with a loud voice, for he is a god; either he is occupied or gone aside, or is on a journey, or perhaps he is asleep and needs to be awakened." So they cried with a loud voice and cut themselves**

according to their custom with swords and lances until the blood gushed out on them.

— 1 Kings 18:27-28

Religion is so *ugly,* and it worships pain and suffering to attract the attention of their deity. Beloved, there is nothing we can do to earn the love of ELOHIM! Yeshua died for us when we were yet sinners! We receive His love by simply turning to *Him* (that is genuine repentance: *Teshuva,* which means "turning to Him and rejecting sin and darkness") and not by trying to harm ourselves or do some "spiritual acrobatics" to attract His attention. Rather than inflicting ourselves with suffering, we need to put our trust in the sufferings of the Messiah as He hanged on the tree (which is the Cross) and took *all* the punishment on Him that you and I deserved. It is only when we put our full trust in what He did (and not on what we can do) that we are truly saved from the wrath to come.

> He made Him who knew no sin to be sin on our behalf, so that we might become the righteousness of God in Him.
>
> — 2 Corinthians 5:21

When true repentance happens, the next phase is getting filled or baptized in His Holy Spirit and Fire.

> "As for me, I baptize you with water for repentance, but He who is coming after me is mightier than I, and I am not fit to remove His sandals; He will baptize you with the Holy Spirit and fire."
>
> — Matthew 3:11

The Baptism of the Holy Spirit and Fire is what separates religion from the true Gospel made in Zion (the original Gospel as handed to the Jewish Apostles 2,000 years ago).

> **But you shall receive power when the Holy Spirit has come upon you; and you shall be witnesses to Me in Jerusalem, and in all Judea and Samaria, and to the end of the earth.**
>
> **— Acts 1:8**

The baptism in the Holy Spirit is so crucial that Yeshua's last instruction to His disciples was to wait in *Yerushalayim* (Jerusalem) until they would receive the power from on High. He did not send them to do *anything* without the power, the anointing of the Ruach HaKodesh (which is the Holy Spirit). The only *key* for receiving this power was to turn to Him or repent from sin unto Him, to be thirsty for Him, to need Him and to want Him. That is all! The rest is His doing.

> **Peter said to them, "Repent, and each of you be baptized in the name of Yeshua the Messiah for the forgiveness of your sins; and you will receive the gift of the Holy Spirit."**
>
> **— Acts 2:38**

When He draws us, we start to hate our sin. Then by our free will, we turn to Him in repentance, forsaking our sins. His Blood cleanses us and makes us righteous before Him, and He fills us with His Holy Spirit and Fire! Everything else will be outcome of being filled with the Holy Spirit and Fire!

Then the Finger of ELOHIM writes the Torah or His instructions in our heart. From that moment, His Ruach

(Spirit) begins to lead us; we only need to *respond*! By our own free will we *choose* to believe, we *choose* to respond, and we *choose* to obey and do what we know to be right in His eyes. But this is a *response* to what He has already done for us. It is a response to His love and Spirit.

No religious system can walk in the Anointing of the Holy Spirit! No, not even the best of Christianity or Judaism can walk in the anointing of the Holy Spirit. The Kingdom of God is not a religious system. Religious systems are established by men to reach a god of their choosing and understanding (see Genesis 11).

THE SPIRITUAL THERMOMETER TEST

The following is a "Spiritual Thermometer." Go ahead and mark any point that you lack in the following list, then you will know what to ask for in prayer.

You can also email us (info@kad-esh.org), and we will direct you to material that can help you and will pray for you to have the fullness of His Gospel, Spirit, and Fire.

ANY GOSPEL THAT DOES NOT CARRY THE FOLLOWING IS NOT THE ORIGINAL GOSPEL:

1. Repentance from sin and iniquity as we have all broken Yah's (God's) Commandments (see Isaiah 53:1-2).
2. Turning to the God of Israel, the Creator of heaven and earth for forgiveness (see Isaiah 45:22).
3. Receiving forgiveness, healing, and deliverance that was purchased by the Blood Sacrifice of the Jewish Messiah Yeshua, thus making Yeshua our King and Savior, Healer, Redeemer, and Deliverer (see Acts 3:16)!

4. Going into the *Mikveh** or the baptismal waters into the name of Yeshua by *full immersion*. Dying to our old way of life and starting a fresh New Life in Him (see Romans 6:4)!
5. Receiving the Baptism or Infilling of the Holy Spirit and Fire either by direct intervention or most often by the laying on of hands of someone else that is filled with the Holy Spirit. It mostly manifests with praying in heavenly languages (tongues) and by an overwhelming presence of Yah (God) (see Deuteronomy 34:9; Acts 2, 19:6).
6. Walking in the anointing and authority of the Holy Spirit in our everyday life, praying in tongues (heavenly languages), manifesting His love and power even in the banalest things of life, healing the sick, and casting out devils in His name (see Mark 16:15-17; Luke 10:19).
7. Responding to this great Salvation with obedience to His Word as revealed by His Spirit (see 2 Corinthians 10:5; Matthew 7:21; John 16:13).
8. Continue to walk with Him in a personal relationship fueled by transparency before Him, prayer, forgiveness (receiving and giving), worship, meditation in His Word, fellowship with other believers, repentance when needed, by faith declaring His Word and promises, in love, in joy, in giving and obedience to His Spirit and will all the days of our life (see Joshua 1:8; Romans 8:13-15; Galatians 5:22-23).
9. Reaching out to others with the same message (see Matthew 28:18-20).

---

* A Jewish ritual immersion for purification and sanctification, normally in a pool or a body of living water; original Biblical baptism.

Therefore, repent and return, so that your sins may be wiped away, in order that times of refreshing may come from the presence of the Lord; and that He may send Yeshua, the Messiah appointed for you.
— Acts 3:19-20

WHY DO REVIVALS DIE?

He who has the seven Spirits of God and the seven stars, says this: 'I know your deeds, that you have a name that you are alive, but you are dead. Wake up, and strengthen the things that remain, which were about to die; for I have not found your deeds completed in the sight of My God. So remember what you have received and heard; and keep it, and repent.
— Revelation 3:1-3

This is the reason why *revivals die*. Even true revivals and genuine outpourings of the Holy Spirit die *because preachers begin to preach their own words rather than His anointed words*. They begin to make human and demonic doctrines that either is not in the Bible at all; or if they are in the Bible, they pervert them according to their fleshly understanding. Then they tend to become either rigid and self-righteous or lax and lukewarm. They preach a cheap grace gospel without any radical faith or obedience, containing no fear of YHVH. Both sides of the pendulum are equally dangerous though the lax and humanistic one "looks better."

We must understand that there is nothing new under the sun! Elohim is the Ancient of Days, and the devil is an old devil, and he uses the same devices again and again.

If we think that we can do something without Yeshua's grace, power, and Holy Spirit anointing, we fool ourselves!

It is the Spirit who gives life; the flesh profits nothing; the words that I have spoken to you are spirit and are life.
— John 6:63

Even if we are preaching the most Scriptural message there is, but there is no *anointing* in the preaching, and if it is not backed up with signs, wonders, and miracles of salvation (healing, deliverance, and restoration), then we are preaching *religion*! If our messages do not bring *conviction* of sin, *repentance,* and *freedom* from lies for people to be transformed by His truth, it is *nothing*! Even if we know all truth, but we have no love, we are nothing! Also, if we sing the most amazingly arranged songs accompanied by the most skilled musicians and professional set-ups, if we have no *anointing,* it is *nothing.*

Knowledge puffs up but love builds up!
— 1 Corinthians 8:1c

Many religious groups have arisen who have discovered that the Church needs to return to its original Jewish roots and foundations. Unfortunately, this discovery has led many to focus on the knowledge while ignoring the love. Most have fallen by the wayside and are no more. This debate has been going on since the 2nd Century. It continued all through the 4th Century when Constantine divorced the Gentile believers from the Jewish Believers and the Gentile Church from Yeshua as the Jewish Messiah grounded in the Torah and Hebrew foundations. All these religious groups and denominations that had the truth given by the Spirit lost the Spirit and the anointing and brought bondage instead of *freedom*.

WHEN THE HOLY SPIRIT ARRIVES, THEN FREEDOM, HEALING, DELIVERANCE, LOVE, JOY, AND EMPOWERMENT COMES

> For what the Law (Torah) could not do, weak as it was through the flesh, God did: sending His own Son in the likeness of sinful flesh and as an offering for sin, He condemned sin in the flesh, so that the requirement of the Law (Torah) might be fulfilled in us, who do not walk according to the flesh but according to the Spirit.
>
> — Romans 8:3-5

Here is His pure grace: That through Yeshua's Blood we have been made righteous to be inhabited by His mighty Holy Spirit! If you are satisfied with the knowledge and more information but have no *anointing* in your life, that knowledge will kill you rather than give *life*. That is why Adam and Eve died spiritually in the Garden of Eden – they chose knowledge rather than presence. They had the presence of ELOHIM with them; His very breath had made them into living beings. But they decided to *know* things without *knowing Him*!

> For our gospel, did not come to you in word only, but also in power and in the Holy Spirit and with full conviction.
>
> — 1 Thessalonians 1:5a

The only way to *know Him* is by the Holy Spirit. There is simply no other way, beloved! Only his Holy Spirit can make

Him known to us, can reveal Him and His Word to us. The letter of the law kills, but the Spirit gives life!

> **Who also made us sufficient as ministers of the new covenant, not of the letter but of the Spirit; for the letter kills, but the Spirit gives life.**
>
> **— 2 Corinthians 3:6**

Knowing His Word without *knowing Him* will bring us to self-righteousness, religion, and death. What precedes the knowledge of the Word-Torah is *knowing Him* by His Ruach (Spirit).

We must have the return of the Holy Spirit, the return of His anointing, Love and Power to our lives, congregations, writings and pulpits.

You see, when we turn to Him and away from sin and receive His awesome forgiveness because of His Blood Sacrifice, we become as a Living Book filled with clean, white pages. Now His Holy Spirit comes to write in the Book of our lives, His Words and ways, His instructions (His written Torah becomes flesh in us as it is interpreted by the revelation of the Holy Spirit).

Preachers must be *very careful* what they preach, because new believers are like that White Book and we need to be careful not to smudge the pages with religious doctrines, like Replacement Theology and others, that bring death rather than life.

Many preachers are like a "broken record" repeating what has been handed down to them without bothering to research for themselves if these things are real.

A CALL TO THE PREACHERS

We need to ask ourselves: Is our preaching producing disciples that are full of the Holy Spirit and Fire, walking in holiness and righteousness and love, displaying the gifts and the fruit of the Spirit?

We preachers need to *turn to Him* once more and become like Clean Books where He can write His Words afresh without the doctrines of demons and men. For His words are Spirit, and they are *life*! If our preaching is the truth and it is anointed by the Holy Spirit, then *fruit* will be seen in our personal lives and our disciples. If not, the gospel that we are preaching does not contain enough truth or power!

> **Beware of false prophets, who come to you in sheep's clothing, but inwardly they are ravenous wolves. You will know them by their fruits. Do men gather grapes from thorn bushes or figs from thistles? Even so, every good tree bears good fruit, but a bad tree bears bad fruit. A good tree cannot bear bad fruit, nor can a bad tree bear good fruit. Every tree that does not bear good fruit is cut down and thrown into the fire. Therefore, by their fruits you will know them.**
>
> **— Matthew 7:15-20**

TURN AFRESH TO HIM

Yeshua, the Jewish Messiah, the Lion of Judah, is inviting us all to *turn* to Him afresh in repentance, receiving His grace and forgiveness in *full*, baptizing us anew in His Holy Spirit and Fire. Then his Words, (not ours or the devil's or men made doctrines and church traditional thinking), can now be written in our hearts, in the Clean Book of our Lives by the indelible Ink of the Holy Spirit.

The Finger of ELOHIM (God), the Holy Spirit, the same one that wrote the Commandments on stones on Mount Sinai, now wants to write His Ways in *living books, living stones*, in you and me.

> You are our epistle written in our hearts, known and read by all men; clearly you are an epistle of Messiah, ministered by us, written not with ink but by the Spirit of the living God, not on tablets of stone but on tablets of flesh, that is, of the heart.
>
> — 2 Corinthians 3: 2-3

Then out of the confusion of a multitude of church doctrines and denominations, there will come a unified voice, a united Bride, a One New Man of Jew and Gentile together as *one*. Then the world will believe! (See John 17:17-21.)

> I do not pray for these alone, but also for those who will believe in Me through their word; that they all may be one, as You, Father, are in Me, and I in You; that they also may be one in Us, that the world may believe that You sent Me.
>
> — John 17:20-21

The way *up* is always *down*! It is humility and repentance that can bring about unity and revival:

> If My People who are called by My name, humble themselves and pray, seek My face and turn from their evil ways, then I will hear from heaven, I will forgive their sin and I will heal their land.
>
> — 2 Chronicles 7:14

Forgive us from our sins and fill us, Abba, with Your Holy Spirit and Fire! Anoint us *one more time*, return us to our first love *one more time*, and make us *one* in your Holy Spirit and Truth, so that Israel and the nations may turn and be saved!

Do not quench the Spirit's Fire.

— 1 Thessalonians 5:19

CHAPTER 4

DRAINING THE SWAMP OF RELIGION

"I will rise up against them," declares the Lord of hosts, "and will cut off from Babylon name and survivors, offspring and posterity," declares YHVH. "I will also make it a possession for the hedgehog and swamps of water, and I will sweep it with the broom of destruction," declares the Lord of hosts.

— *Isaiah 14:22-23*

I can't think of a more important task than to drain the swamp of religion. To understand the whole thing, let us see what "swamp" means and then what exactly is "religion."

The simple definition of a swamp, from the Merriam Webster dictionary online:

1. a wetland often partially or intermittently covered with water, especially one dominated by woody vegetation
2. a tract of swamp
3. a difficult or troublesome situation or subject

Swamps are stagnant waters that form their own ecosystem, which includes all kinds of insects and animals that can be dangerous if left unchecked. *One such insect is the Anopheles mosquito that carries the terrible disease of Malaria.*

Some of the swamps have muddy areas and sinkholes that are so deep they can suck an individual into it when an attempt is made to walk through them. Though today society loves to protect swamps as nature reserves, we need to realize that in essence, a swamp can be quite dangerous, albeit intriguing and exciting to the nature researcher.

Before the establishing of the State of Israel, young Jewish pioneers worked diligently at draining the malaria-infested swamps in the north of Israel.

About 70-80 percent of these sacrificial Jews died of malaria. They cleared up the entire Galilee region, making it possible to develop agriculture and to eradicate malaria from the Land. The Nature's Defense Society in Israel has left one small swamp as a Nature Reserve. It is called *Yamat Hachula*, in the upper Galilee not far from the Lebanese border.

The connection between *malaria* and *swamps* was known even in ancient times. Evil spirits or malaria gods were believed to live within the marshes.

The association with stagnant waters (breeding grounds for Anopheles) led the Romans to begin drainage programs, the first intervention against malaria.

It is said that Emperor Nero drained the swamps near ancient Rome, to rid the city of malaria. By the Middle Ages, kings and feudal lords feared marshes as breeding grounds of plagues and incurable fevers; as a result, a royal decree was passed in 11th Century Valencia, sentencing any farmer to death who planted rice too close to villages and towns. In Britain, the 'Roman technology' of draining swamps protected some areas from malaria during this time. Italian physician Lancisi in 1717 had suggested a possible role for mosquitoes in transmission of malaria and proposed the draining of marshes to eradicate malaria.

Ronald Ross's discovery of Anopheles mosquito as the vector for malaria in 1897 opened a new chapter in malaria control. Ross attempted to eradicate malaria from England by forming 'mosquito brigades' to eliminate mosquito larvae from stagnant pools and marshes. Because he had very limited funding, the best available technology was to pour oil on the numerous breeding sites around Freetown. As soon as the oil treatments stopped, breeding would begin again.

Malaria's decline in the United States and Europe in the late 1800s was due mainly to draining swamps and removing mill ponds.

Draining swamps also exposed good agricultural land, enabling people to afford better houses and thus isolate the sick. In 1998 Dr. Gro Harlem Brundtland, Director-General of the World Health Organization, launched a worldwide Roll Back Malaria (RBM) Initiative against malaria. The RBM Strategy included early case detection and prompt treatment, integrated vector management and Containment of focal epidemics. However, the program is far from being successful.

Today, it's a much worse scenario. Thoughtless man-made irrigation schemes and dams provided new habitats for Anopheles and resulted in 'man-made' malaria.

The extension of urban areas leads to epidemics in the peripheries of the growing cities. Mass migrations of non-immune populations into endemic areas for political reasons has further complicated matters. More than 300 million cases have resulted in 2 million deaths. We see multi-insecticide and multi-drug resistance, non-use of DDT, and non-availability of cheap, effective chemo-therapeutics and prophylactics. Now a steady-state, benign holoendemic malaria is replaced by unstable hyperendemicity. Functional immunity is impaired by the ad hoc chemotherapy distributed from the primary health centers: this is déjà vu all over again.

New technology promises to bring the always-in-the-pipeline vaccine and the more flashy bed nets dipped in permethrin. The super-sensitive, single-minded

Ross went to his grave still holding the firm conviction that malaria could be eradicated if only weak-willed governments would commit themselves to exploit his discovery and attack the anopheline in their watery lairs. (Malariasite.com)

Draining of swamps has been the most consistent and successful treatment against malaria and the only one that eradicates it altogether.

We can also see that "oil treatment" onto the infested waters can stop the disease if continued but cannot eradicate it altogether. Please remember this fact as I keep on unveiling the subject of this chapter.

WHAT IS RELIGION? AND WHAT IS A RELIGIOUS SWAMP?

Religion is defined as:

- the belief in and worship of a superhuman controlling power, especially a personal God or gods
- "ideas about the relationship between science and religion"
- a particular system of faith and worship.
- *Synonyms:* faith, belief, divinity, worship, creed, teaching, doctrine, theology
- plural noun: *religions* – "the world's great religions"
- a pursuit or interest to which someone ascribes supreme importance – "consumerism is the new religion"

We can see that though "religion" could mean the belief in one God that created the universe with absolute laws and principles, it does not necessarily mean that.

Anything that you worship can be your religion. Religion can be all-inclusive (like New Age and the Interfaith Movement) or exclusive (like many cults as the Mooney and others). We need to establish here that the author of religion is man and not ELOHIM-God the Creator. The first religious system and religious building is the City of Babel (as described in Genesis 11).

> They said, "Come, let us build for ourselves a city, and a tower whose top will reach into heaven, and let us make for ourselves a name, otherwise we will be scattered abroad over the face of the whole earth."
>
> — Genesis 11:4

The Almighty was not pleased, and He came down to confuse their languages so they could not go on building.

> Therefore its name was called Babel, because there YHVH confused the language of the whole earth; and from there YHVH scattered them abroad over the face of the whole earth.
>
> — Genesis 11:9

About 2,000 years ago, the Creator of the Universe (YHVH and the God of Israel) sent His Jewish Son and Messiah to pay the price that we owed Him.

All of humanity had been estranged from Him, and He sought to reconcile us to Himself. This reconciliation could not happen by our own establishing of religious buildings or systems but requires us to humble ourselves to return to Him. We could only return to Him if justice could be satisfied and forgiveness could follow. This Jewish Son and Messiah by the name of Yeshua—which means "Salvation"—died though He was innocent, at the hands of Roman soldiers, who nailed Him to a Roman execution cross, accusing Him of being the King of the Jews.

He was like an innocent Lamb slaughtered by the Romans in the time of the Biblical-Hebrew Feast of Passover. The spilling of His innocent blood was the atonement needed to cleanse the earth and man from sin and its deathly outcome. Whoever would believe in the Jewish Savior Yeshua, could now be reconciled with His Father, the Creator of the Universe. It was possible now to begin to live on this earth in purity, righteousness, and blessing, including the promise of spending all of eternity in His Kingdom. Such believers would now follow the principles of the Creator and His Ways – by meditating on the Torah (the Holy Scriptures as given to the people of Israel) and by being filled with the presence, the Spirit of ELOHIM the Creator (the Holy Spirit, Fire, or the Ruach HaKodesh). These believers would change the world!

Unfortunately, about 300 years after Yeshua lived, died and rose from the dead a religious system was built, replacing the original faith delivered to the first Jewish Disciples.

A kind of Babel was built by men and authorities in the Roman Empire, making it illegal to believe according to the original faith. *A "Religious Swamp" began to be formed – with stagnation and with all kinds of deadly doctrines of demons and men – which can be likened unto the mosquitos of Malaria.* This religious system, coupled with majestic buildings and elaborate feasts borrowed from paganism, was called "Christianity." It developed as imperial, conquering religion bringing with it spiritual malaria from a demonic doctrine called Replacement Theology. This theology sought to replace all the original Messianic faith as handed to the Jewish Believers 2,000 years ago. Wherever this imperial Christianity went it left people spiritually sick or dead – it brought spiritual rape, slavery, and murder.

The Swamp of Replacement Theology Christianity has killed more people than the malaria-infested swamps of the world.

The only hope for humanity is to drain this religious swamp altogether so that good fruit-bearing ground can be formed in the hearts of the believers in the Jewish Messiah Yeshua (whom many erroneously call Jesus Christ). As long as the swamp of religion is not fully drained, the sporadic "oil treatments" and Holy Spirit renewals will not be able to solve this problem that is stopping revival and awakening all over the world: Including the forming of Sheep Nations.

THE TIME HAS COME TO DRAIN THE SWAMP OF REPLACEMENT THEOLOGY!

> Yeshua said to him, "I am the way, and the truth, and the life; no one comes to the Father but through Me."
>
> — John 14:6

CHAPTER 5

RESTORING THE GOSPEL MADE IN ZION
GOING BACK TO THE WAY

> Yeshua said to him, "I am the way, the truth, and the life! No one comes to the Father except through Me. If you have come to know Me (the Jewish Messiah), you will know My Father also. From now on, you do know Him and have seen Him."
>
> — *John 14:6-7*

𝓗ERE WE WILL understand the Biblical Gospel, the one made in Zion, as defined by:

1. Its source: The Torah (Laws and Instructions of God), the Prophets and the Writings. These are known altogether as the *Tanakh* or the Holy Scriptures—wrongly called 'Old Testament' (Jeremiah 31:31-34; Isaiah 53; Isaiah 61; and many more).

2. Its fathers: The Jewish people.
3. The culture in which it developed: A Jewish-Hebrew culture.
4. The Land in which it was born: The Holy Land of Israel including Galilee, Jerusalem, and Judea
5. Its central figure: The Jewish Messiah, Yeshua, born from the House of King David in the Jewish City of *Beth Lechem* (Bethlehem, "The House of Bread").
6. Its first Messengers that spread the Good News: 12 Jewish apostles and numerous Jewish disciples.
7. Its first Congregation of Believers: In the Holy City of Jerusalem, the eternal Capital of Israel.
8. The name of this group of believers and disciples of the Jewish Messiah: "The Way," or in Hebrew *HaDerekh* (based on John 14:6).

THE CONTENT OF THE BIBLICAL GOSPEL

Contrary to what many believe today, the contents of the *Biblical Gospel* (the true Gospel made in Zion) is first and foremost, found in the *Tanakh* – the Hebrew Holy Scriptures wrongly termed 'Old Testament.' The New Covenant is found in this Holy Book, which is its eternal foundation and blueprint. The New Testament portion of the Bible *cannot stand* without the words given to Moses, and all the Prophets of Israel recorded in the *Tanakh*.

All the Jewish Apostles (including Paul, that wrote significant parts of what we call the New Testament today) and *all* the Disciples did not have the New Testament for nearly 300 years! Their source of information and instruction was the Torah (Laws and Instructions); *Neviim* (Prophets); *Ketuvim*

(Writings such as Psalms and Proverbs). The *Tanakh* is what they studied, and this is the text from which they preached.

It is historically accurate that the *Biblical Gospel* advanced especially strong throughout the First Century until the death of the last Jewish apostle. Then in the 2nd Century, great pagan beliefs became mixed in, which affected believers until the Great Falling Away and Apostasy of the 4th Century. In the year 325 A.D. the New Testament was canonized by the Gentile Church fathers to replace the *Tanakh*, the Hebrew Holy Scriptures. They labeled it the "Old Testament" and declared it virtually obsolete and useless. From then on preachers used mostly the New Testament to make doctrine and may have even tampered with some of its portions. (note: It is believed that the Book of Matthew was written in Hebrew and its original is still in the Vatican.) This resulted in giving our teachings an anti-Jewish slant to support "the divorce from anything Jewish" according to the Council of Nicaea, signed in year 325 A.D. as well.

The Council of Nicaea and the New Testament were now adopted instead of the *Tanakh*, which had been guiding and directing all the Jewish Apostles and Disciples of the First Century. It is about the importance of the Hebrew Scriptures that Paul the *Shaliach* (Messenger or Apostle) said the following to Timothy, his son in the faith:

> ... and that from childhood you have known the sacred writings that are able to make you wise, leading to salvation through trusting in Messiah Yeshua. All Scripture is inspired by God and useful for teaching, for reproof, for restoration, and for training in

righteousness, so that the person belonging to God may be capable, fully equipped for every good deed.

— 2 Timothy 3:15-17

Keep in mind that there was no New Testament when he spoke these words – so the "*all* scripture" Paul talks about here is precisely that which was *discarded* in year 325 by the Gentile Church Fathers as 'Old Testament.' Paul would not have agreed with this at all! In fact, the New Testament carries historical recounts of Yeshua's Life, death, burial, and resurrection from four different eyewitnesses called the Gospels. These are followed by the Book of Acts written by Luke (probably the only Gentile that contributed to the New Testament). Then we have the letters of Paul, Peter, John, and *Ya'akov* (James) written to their disciples, culminating with the Book of Revelation when Yeshua powerfully revealed Himself to *Yochanan* (John), the Jewish Apostle on the Isle of Patmos (based on a supernatural visitation of the Messiah).

While all of these books are extremely important and deserve a place of honor, they *cannot* replace the Holy Scriptures, the *Tanakh* which Paul instructed Timothy to learn from – to preach and to teach from. From year 325 A.D. until the present day, the *Biblical Gospel* was replaced by the cultural Gospel of Rome. *Another Gospel* came into the Body of Believers, and with it came its ensuing *curse*.

But even if we (or an angel from heaven) should announce any "good news" to you other than what we have proclaimed to you, let that person be cursed! As we have said before, so I now repeat: if

anyone proclaims to you "good news" other than what you received, let that person be under a curse! Am I now trying to win people's approval, or God's? Or am I trying to please people? If I were still trying to please people, I would not be a servant of Messiah.

— Galatians 1:8-10

This *other, foreign* gospel was followed mainly by Gentiles. Jews were forbidden from being Jewish anymore or from practicing the Torah in the Spirit lifestyle that Paul and all the other Jewish and Gentile disciples of the First Century practiced—including Cornelius with his family and friends, Lydia, Apollos and more. When this *other* Gospel or the cultural Gospel came in with its Roman customs, pagan feasts and traditions, those among the Jewish believers (and only a few of the Gentile believers that opposed it) became anathema and went into hiding. Eventually, terrible persecutions and murders began to happen against anyone that had a "trace" of Jewishness or Biblical traditions in them, such as celebrating Shabbat or the Biblical Feasts, honoring the Dietary Commandments in Leviticus 11 or other instructions from the Torah. Even having any relationship with Jews was forbidden. Those were termed Judaizers and were severely punished – some also burnt at the stake by the cultural Church of Rome, Spain, and Europe.

From the 4th Century until our day, the *Biblical Gospel* coming from Israel (through the Jewish people, from whom came the Jewish Messiah) became forbidden. We even lost the original name that the Father in heaven called the Jewish

Messiah, His Divine Son. His God-given name denoted his Hebrew origins - *Yeshua*, meaning "salvation."

THE BIBLICAL GOSPEL BELIEVERS

The People of the Way went into hiding from the cultural Gospel believers (the Christians, the adherents of a Roman-based religion called "Christianity"; together with their Romanized Savior by the name of Jesus Christ, who bears no resemblance at all to the Jewish Messiah Yeshua). Countless images, icons and pictures will now be made by the cultural Gospel Church (Orthodox and Catholic) that will now portray a gentile/Christian savior hanging on the cross with a short beard, light eyes – and many times looking weak and effeminate.

Together with this reforming of our Savior came the exaltation of His Mother Mary (instead of the real Jewish *Miriam*). They began to worship Mary in various forms. Virgin worship and veneration, as many call it, became a solid pillar of the cultural Gospel Church, thus violating the first of the 10 Commandments as given to the people of Israel:

> You shall not have other gods beside Me. 'Do not make for yourself a graven image— no image of what is in the heavens above or on the earth beneath or in the water under the earth. Do not bow down to them or worship them. For I, ADONAI your God, am a jealous God, visiting the iniquity of the fathers on the children and on the third and fourth generation of those who hate Me, but showing loving-kindness to a thousand generations of those who love Me and keep My mitzvoth (commandments).
>
> — Deuteronomy 5:7-10

That practice also opposes these essential words in the New Testament:

> For there is one God and one mediator also between God and men - the man Messiah Yeshua.
>
> — 1 Timothy 2:5

> Yeshua said to him, "I am the way, the truth, and the life! No one comes to the Father except through Me. If you have come to know Me (the Jewish Messiah!), you will know My Father also. From now on, you do know Him and have seen Him."
>
> — John 14:6-7

> Then one of the elders tells me, "Stop weeping! Behold, the Lion of the tribe of Judah (The Jewish Lion!), the Root of David, has triumphed—He is worthy to open the scroll and its seven seals."
>
> — Revelation 5:5

A CULTURAL UNBIBLICAL CALENDAR

On top of the rejection to all the Jewish roots and Hebrew Biblical foundations of faith, this Apostate Church preaching another gospel adopted Greco-Roman pagan celebrations. They even kept the same dates that commemorated celebrations of foreign deities, along with some of their traditions but gave these unholy feasts a Pseudo-Biblical Christian context. This *paganism* is how Sunday, the day of worship of Jupiter (their Sun-god) replaces the Holy Shabbat—the 7th Day set apart from creation by our Creator as the Day of Rest forever. Yah gave it as a sign and mark to the people of Israel to keep and teach the nations about it. (See Genesis 2; Exodus 31; Isaiah 56.)

This paganism is also how Easter (the celebration of the goddess of fertility and procreation *Ishtar*) is introduced to replace Passover. During that time, she was worshiped through orgies between women and priests at the temple of *Ishtar* from which babies were conceived and born. A portion of those babies was then sacrificed to the goddess in thanksgiving the following year during Easter celebration.

The tradition was that eggs would then be dipped in the blood of the slaughtered babies and were proudly displayed before all to see. Now, Easter would be dressed by the cultural Church as a 'holy feast,' and the eggs would become a cherished tradition as we enjoy our "painted Easter eggs." This is bringing *a curse* upon babies and children, as written by the Prophet Hosea:

> **My people are destroyed for lack of knowledge. Since you rejected knowledge, I will also reject you from being My kohen (priest). Since you forgot the Torah of your God, just so I will forget your children.**
> **— Hosea 4:6**

Christmas crept in the same way, to celebrate the birth of Jesus Christ – at a time when Yeshua the Jewish Messiah could not be born. He was most probably born in *Sukkot*, the Fall Feast of Booths. But it was a convenient time to control the Roman masses that grew restless in the long winter months and needed something to cheer them up.

The Romanized cultural Church adopted the winter witchcraft solstice (the shortest day in the secular calendar year) when people celebrated the birth of the "Unconquered Sun" or Jupiter through a Feast named *Saturnalia* later renamed "Christ-Mass" or a Mass Service for Christ's birth. It was customary to give gifts to each other, to dance around evergreen trees especially reserved for the occasion and to decorate them. There is a host of Christmas traditions like kissing under the mistletoe and the figure of Santa Claus, a derivative of the Nordic god of violence—Thor (that came in much later) or "Satan Claws" that are all pagan. And yet the Church today; *both* Catholics, Protestants, Evangelicals and even Pseudo-Messianics celebrate them or tolerate them as "holy" or at least "acceptable."

BUT IS IT ACCEPTABLE TO THE ALMIGHTY?

> Then He brought me into the inner court of the Lord's house. And behold, at the entrance to the temple of the Lord, between the porch and the altar, were about twenty-five men with their backs to the temple of the Lord and their faces toward the east; and they were prostrating themselves eastward toward the sun.
>
> — Ezekiel 8:16

All of the Christian celebrations including Sunday worship, Easter, Resurrection Sunday, Christmas, and Halloween or All Saints Day come from Sun Worship!

Why would anyone that genuinely loves the God of Israel and the Jewish Messiah Yeshua want to keep them or defend them? Is it because they love the cultural Gospel more than the *Biblical Gospel* and their socially acceptable traditions more than the Creator? Why is it that many pastors and teachers that know the Truth are still unwilling to teach it to their congregations, fearing they lose members? Why would they prefer their "numbers" rather than pleasing the Living God? Do they really care for the sheep that are perishing in their ignorance then? And if they dismiss these questions and remarks as "radical" and "extreme," *who* are they really dismissing?

See a description of the Christmas Tree in the Holy Scriptures:

> **Thus says A**DONAI**: "Do not learn the way of the nations or be frightened by signs of the heavens—though the nations are terrified by them. The customs of the peoples are useless: it is just a tree cut from the forest, the work of the hands of a craftsman with a chisel. They decorate it with silver and gold and fasten it with hammer and nails so it won't totter."**
>
> **— Jeremiah 10:2-4**

CHRISTMAS TREES ARE IDOLS ON THE ALTARS OF MANY CHURCHES OF ALL DENOMINATIONS!

Christmas trees are reminiscent of sun worship and non-acceptable by the God of the Bible. The reason for the tradition is that the Church at large, not only the Catholics, are still steeped in the cultural Gospel and not in the *Biblical Gospel*.

Now in the Third Millennium, if we do not return back to the *Biblical Gospel* made in Zion, to the Jewish Messiah Yeshua and to the same doctrine of the Jewish Apostles of the Way, we will surely die. *The curse promised to those who preach "another gospel" has reached its climax, and Yeshua wants His Bride back from the cultural Gospel of Christianity – Catholic, Protestant, and Evangelical, those of every denomination.*

THE BIBLICAL GOSPEL DISCIPLES CARRY THE MARK OF YESHUA – THE WAY

1. They have the Baptism of the Holy Spirit and Fire.
2. They have anointing and authority followed with signs, wonders, and miracles.
3. They have an intimate, personal, and sacrificial walk of love and obedience with the Jewish Messiah led by His Holy Spirit.
4. They live a Biblical Torah based lifestyle of nonreligious holiness and righteousness.
5. They keep Shabbat and the Biblical Feasts as described in Leviticus 23.
6. They make Disciples instead of "converts," "numbers," or "decisions."
7. They love, honor, and stand with Israel – the Mother of the Nations and the vessel chosen by Yah (God) to bring the *Biblical Gospel* to the world. With the return of Messiah, these people will rule and reign from, yes, their Capital Jerusalem for 1,000 years.

Many nations will join themselves to YHVH in that day and will become My people. Then I will dwell in your midst, and you will know that YHVH of hosts has sent Me to you. YHVH will possess Judah as His portion in the holy land and will again choose Jerusalem. Be silent, all flesh, before YHVH; for He is aroused from His holy habitation.

— Zechariah 2:11-13

CHAPTER 6

THE SECOND EXODUS
LEAVING THE CULTURAL GOSPEL

> Then I heard another voice from heaven saying,
> "Come out of her, my people, lest you participate
> in her sins and receive her plagues!
>
> — *Revelation 18:4*

THIS PASSOVER FEAST and season mark a divine command for a great exodus out of the religious system called "*the Cultural Gospel*."

What is a Cultural Gospel? It is precisely the opposite of the Gospel of the Kingdom, or what I call the Biblical Gospel.

THE TRUE BIBLICAL GOSPEL IS:
1. Followed and demonstrated with signs, wonders, and miracles (see Acts 1 and 2; Mark 16:15-17; throughout the Book of Acts).
2. Identified with standards that are in direct confrontation with this world's system (see Luke 12:49-53; Matthew 5:17-21).
3. Where people are distinctively different/holy/set apart from the rest of society (see 1 Peter 2:9; John 12:25).
4. Risky and unpopular because it's so different than what most people think or believe.

The keyword here is *different/holy/set-apart*, but not unapproachable and uncaring. (John 3:19)

The equivalent natural element is *salt* – people can take a little bit and then become thirsty for *water*, but no one can eat it by the spoonful.

> You are the salt of the earth; but if the salt should lose its flavor, how shall it be made salty again? It is no longer good for anything, except to be thrown out and trampled under foot by men.
> — Matthew 5:13

THE CULTURAL GOSPEL IS:
1. Reasonable, logical, and non-confronting.
2. All-inclusive and adjusts to this world's system in a religious way.
3. One that causes people to become socially popular – ones that blend in.

4. Palatable and acceptable.

The keyword here is *popular*/palatable/acceptable/well-liked. The equivalent natural element is *sugar*: The more you eat, the more addictive it becomes until you never seem to have enough to satisfy you. In actuality you are malnourished, which makes you crave it even more. Then the more you eat, the worse your immune system becomes – your heart and entire cell system become weak and sick. Very often Cancer begins to creep in unnoticed!

When the Gospel is preached without the Baptism of the Holy Spirit and Fire, it becomes either poisonous sugar ("cheap grace" religion) or bitter poison (rigid religion). Billy Graham preached on salvation but did not endorse the Baptism in the Holy Spirit (with speaking in tongues and the gifts of the Spirit) which makes people radically different! He preached about the Gospel and the importance of the Word, but most of the time his Bible was only a New Testament – not the whole Bible. The New Testament was canonized in the 4th Century and then added to the Hebrew Holy Scriptures (which many label as "Old Testament"). *The New Testament cannot stand on its own without the original Hebrew foundation: The Torah, Prophets and the Writings – and without the Baptism in the Holy Spirit.*

A Gospel that is preached without Torah and Spirit is a *cultural gospel* that becomes acceptable to the masses. This aligns with what happened in the 4th Century (from 325 A.D.) when Roman leadership legalized the Cultural Gospel, thus we were divorced from the true Biblical Gospel. Billy Graham has spent nearly seven decades preaching the Cultural Gospel to America and many nations, but the USA is not any better for it. According to a report dated the 9th of March 2018, written by White House Correspondent William Koenig, only *one* percent (1%) of the children in the USA have a Biblical World view!*

This statistic indicates that 99% of these children are destined to grow into anti-Biblical adults unless something radically different than Billy Graham happens in America. And not only in America but in all nations! Billy did the best with what he knew (or chose to know) and was very successful in his ministry. But *this is the fruit* of what happened to the USA while he was regarded as the pastor of the presidents and the people: *We have lost 99% of the children*! Not to mention the millions of aborted babies! I am sure he meant well and that he agonized over America's condition. But he was limited by the Cultural Gospel that he knew – perhaps he refused to listen to the Shofar call that was beckoning him and all Christians to return home to the Gospel Made in Zion. This question will remain a mystery for the time being.

Billy, as well as most well-intentioned Christians, have been the product of the Cultural Gospel that was adopted by Rome through the Council of Nicaea in 325 A.D. This Cultural gospel replaced the original Gospel coming out of Zion through the Jewish Apostles 2,000 years ago – it replaced Israel, the Torah, the Biblical Celebrations and the Baptism of the Holy Spirit for that which would please the masses.

---

* https://www.watch.org/subscribers/koenigs-eye-view/article/38281

Every Move of Yah (God) since the 16th Century has tried to restore what was lost. But since the 20th Century, something has halted the restoration, and no significant advances have been made. I believe that from 1998, the Jubilee of the State of Israel, the Almighty has been calling the Church out of this Cultural-Replacement Theology Gospel and back to *the Biblical Gospel made in Zion* (with Torah, Biblical Feasts, Holy Spirit Fire, signs, wonders and miracles).

Most of those in the Charismatic Movement and the Prophetic Movement fell asleep on their laurels because of pride in past revivals, refusing to listen to the Shofar sound telling them to return home to the Gospel made in Zion and to renounce *all* Replacement Theology! Because of this, the Evangelical Cultural Gospel represented by Billy Graham took over the USA and the nations. Consequently, without Torah as a foundation or the honoring of Biblical Feasts there has been no demonstration of the Holy Spirit's real power, as described in the Book of Acts of the (Jewish) Apostles!

Now we are about to enter into the 70th Anniversary of the State of Israel (this May, before *Shavuot* /Pentecost). The Almighty is giving a final call before severe judgment falls on His House, the Church at large. This is the *last call for a Great Exodus out of the Cultural Gospel,* and this last call is ratified by the death of the greatest evangelist that ever lived, Reverend Billy Graham. This death has marked *the end of grace for the Cultural Gospel* and the Global thrusting of the Messianic Apostolic Prophetic Revolution (MAP).

I have been warning about this since my first seminar titled *Back to the Roots* in *Herisau*, Switzerland, along with the first publication of my book *The Healing Power of the Roots* in 1993. It was at that time when Abba said that preaching about the Jewish roots of the faith was "a matter of life and death." He said that the Church was like a rose cut off from her garden and put into a vase of water for two days (one day is like 1,000 years to ADONAI). And if she is not replanted back on the Third Day she will surely die!*

In the USA alone, with 140 million Christians, it is estimated that 100 million are steeped in Replacement Theology – having nothing to do with Israel besides claiming her promises for themselves. Most of them endorse homosexuality as an acceptable lifestyle. That is about 2/3 of all Christians in the USA: the friend of Israel! Imagine what happens in other countries!**

There will be a Happy Passover to all that leave the Cultural Gospel behind (with all its Replacement Theologies) and return home to the Biblical Gospel made in Zion, including a Biblical lifestyle—one followed with signs, wonders, and miracles!

> **Therefore, let us celebrate the feast, not with old leaven, nor with the leaven of malice and wickedness, but with the unleavened bread of sincerity and truth.**
>
> **— 1 Corinthians 5:8**

---

*   The key for replanting the rose is studying our *GRM Bible School*: www.grmbibleschool.com.

**   https://www.watch.org/subscribers/koenigs-eye-view/article/38281

CHAPTER 7

THE THIRD DAY REVIVAL

Create in me a clean heart, O God, and renew a steadfast spirit within me. Do not cast me away from Your presence, and do not take Your Holy Spirit from me.

— Psalm 51:10-11

---

*T*HE REVIVAL OF THE THIRD DAY calls us to return to Him, to Yeshua the Jewish Messiah and to the love and honor of the Jewish people, the Israel of today who is the Mother of the Nations. Yeshua is calling us to lay down our weapons, our lies and arrogance, to lay down all strife and seek Him. Only He can restore us as we repent from all personal sins and doctrinal lies. We must seek Him.*

* Download our free booklet here: https://kad-esh.org/shop/third-day-revival-ebook/

THE BIRTH OF THE MESSIANIC MOVEMENT

The Messianic Jewish Movement was born in the '60s. Jews no longer had to stop being Jewish to believe in the Jewish Messiah. Up until this time, a Jew could only recognize Jesus Christ and Christianity if they wanted to embrace the gospel and salvation. They had to forsake Shabbat and Biblical Feasts, the Dietary Commandments and now join the Christians on Sunday, celebrating Christmas and Easter, and start eating pork to show they were really saved. When this Messianic Jewish Movement started it was revolutionary! Jews could remain Jews and worship the Jewish Jesus—or rather Yeshua the Jewish Messiah through Shabbat and Biblical Feasts. And finally, they were not required to eat pork to show "freedom from the law."

> "Do not think that I came to abolish the Torah or the Prophets! I did not come to abolish, but to fulfill. Amen, I tell you, until heaven and earth pass away, not the smallest letter or serif shall ever pass away from the Torah until all things come to pass. Therefore, whoever breaks one of the least of these commandments, and teaches others the same, shall be called least in the kingdom of heaven. But whoever keeps and teaches them, this one shall be called great in the kingdom of heaven. For I tell you that unless your righteousness exceeds that of the Pharisees and Torah scholars, you shall never enter the kingdom of heaven!
> — Matthew 5:17-20

Many Gentiles were being attracted to their messianic synagogues, but they were not always welcomed and encouraged. The new Jewish believers were wary of Christians and Christianity, and they did not want the Gentile believers to take over their congregations (because they were more in numbers than the Jewish believers). This had happened in the past when the Gentiles took over: It led to Replacement Theology, the Council of Nicaea by Emperor Constantine and the Gentile Church Fathers showing hatred against the Jews, resulting in humiliation and genocide.

GENTILE MESSIANIC CONGREGATIONS

A brother offended is harder to be won than a strong city, and contentions are like the bars of a citadel.
— Proverbs 18:19

Many of the Gentile Christians felt rejected in the Messianic Jewish congregations, and they began to form their own Gentile Messianic groups, mostly without any Jews. Out of this woundedness, the Two-House Movement started, claiming that all the Gentile Christians that wanted to follow Torah are the House of Ephraim or the House of Israel.

Some of them went as far as trying to make *Aliyah** by claiming their "Ephraimite natural heritage," only to be rejected shamefully by the Israeli authorities.

Two Messianic camps were formed that were hostile to each other: Messianic Jews, with their own ministry associations; and the Two-House Messianic camp that have their own ministry organizations.

---

* Literally: Ascension; referring to going up to Jerusalem (Zion), meaning *"immigration to Israel."*

The Two-House Movement is a type of Replacement Theology which carries a grudge, a bitter judgment against the Messianic Jews that rejected them out of suspicion and fear. It bears little fruit. On the other hand, many Messianic Jewish synagogues have dried up spiritually and have lost the anointing because of their suspicion of "all things Christian"— they put the baptism in the Holy Spirit (with speaking in tongues) and the move of the Spirit in that mix. Things are not well on both sides of the spectrum. This way is far from the fulfillment of John 17 and the prayer that Yeshua prayed concerning *unity*.

THE MESSIANIC APOSTOLIC PROPHETIC (MAP) MOVEMENT

Repent, therefore, and return—so your sins might be blotted out, so times of relief might come from the presence of Adonai and He might send Yeshua, the Messiah appointed for you. heaven must receive Him, until the time of the restoration of all the things that God spoke about long ago through the mouth of His holy prophets.

— Acts 3:19-21

In the midst of this seeming chaos and hostility between the two Messianic camps, YHVH was doing something to break down the walls (between Jew and Gentile, black and white, male and female) and to advance His master plan: For the natural and spiritual restoration of Israel and for the forming of Sheep Nations. These would be "the fullness of the Gentiles" promised to Ephraim by Jacob.

But these believers in Messiah would not come in angry or claiming "Ephraimite identity" and equal rights to the Land of the Jews. These non-Jewish believers would humbly and repentantly become grafted into the Olive Tree, drinking from the same rich root which the people of Israel were given (the Torah). They would not claim to be "the prodigal or the lost brother," which became the *motto* of the Two-House movement. No! They would instead *unite* with Israel in heart, as a Ruth to a Naomi – and they would perform acts of repentance and restitution for the sins committed by Christians and Christianity against the Jews in the name of Jesus Christ.

The Messianic Apostolic Prophetic (MAP) Revolution was born in 1993 with the release of my book, The Healing Power of the Roots, *calling all Christians to repentance for the ravages and the results of Replacement Theology.*

This Revolution espoused the restoration of Shabbat, the Feasts and Torah as anointed by the Holy Spirit, as well as a walk of humility and sacrifice towards the Jewish people – regarding them as Mother Israel and not as "our elder brother."

Now Messianic Jews and Messianic Gentiles could become *one* as Yeshua had prayed 2,000 years ago. The *One New Man* Body of Messiah began to be formed by the Power of the Spirit of Truth in Love.

> **Sanctify them in the truth; Your word is truth; "I do not ask on behalf of these alone, but for those (Gentiles) also who believe in Me through their word (the word of the Jewish disciples) that they may all be one; even as You, Father, are in Me and I in You, that they also may be in Us, so that the world may believe that You sent Me."**
>
> **— John 17:17, 20-21**

THE EPHRAIM CONTROVERSY

It is time to put to rest a controversy that has caused much pain to the heart of the Father, and this I will call as the "Ephraimite Controversy." It is based on the passage of Scripture below.

> When Joseph saw his father placing his right hand on Ephraim's head he was displeased; so he took hold of his father's hand to move it from Ephraim's head to Manasseh's head. Joseph said to him, "No, my father, this one is the firstborn; put your right hand on his head." But his father refused and said, "I know, my son, I know. He too will become a people, and he too will become great. Nevertheless, his younger brother will be greater than he, and his descendants will become the fullness of the gentile nations." He blessed them that day and said, "In your name will Israel pronounce this blessing: 'May God make you like Ephraim and Manasseh.'" So he put Ephraim ahead of Manasseh.
>
> — Genesis 48:17-20

Ephraim, the younger son of Joseph, Son of Ya'akov, was going to become a group of nations that is called the *fullness of the Gentiles,* and I will call it *"Sheep Nations."* This would be accomplished by a massive exile of the Northern Kingdom of Israel, called the House of Israel or Ephraim during the 8th Century B.C. Many people call them "The 10 Lost Tribes." They were exiled to the different parts of the Assyrian Empire, so the tribes and families were divided and scattered, and they disappeared into the nations until this day. By mixing with the nations they would now become the fullness of the *Goyim* or *the fullness of the Gentiles. Not the fullness of Israel!*

These Gentile-Israelite mixtures would be the fulfillment of the Promise given to Abraham that he would become the father of many nations (besides the Nation of Israel).

> For this reason it is by faith, in order that it may be in accordance with grace, so that the promise will be guaranteed to all the descendants, not only to those who are of the Torah, but also to those who are of the faith of Abraham, who is the father of us all, (as it is written, "A father of many nations have I made you") in the presence of Him whom he believed, even God, who gives life to the dead and calls into being that which does not exist. In hope against hope he believed, so that he might become a father of many nations according to that which had been spoken, "So shall your descendants be."
>
> — Romans 4:16-18

This fullness of the Gentiles would be judged on how they treated the least of the Jewish brethren of Yeshua.

> All the (Gentiles-*Goyim*) nations will be gathered before Him; and He will separate them from one another, as the shepherd separates the sheep from the goats; and He will put the sheep on His right, and the goats on the left.
>
> — Matthew 25:32-33

> (Pointing to His Jewish disciples) The King will answer and say to them, 'Truly I say to you, to the extent that you did it to one of these brothers of Mine, even the least of them, you did it to Me.'
>
> — Matthew 25:40

Sheep Nations could not happen by claiming Ephraimite or "House of Israel" identity but by standing and blessing the Jewish people in their time of need. Ephraim—or the House of Israel—was exiled and mixed with the nations *until they could not be recognized as Israelites anymore.*

Then through the Blood of Yeshua, their descendants now completely gentilized and not of "pure Israelite blood" will be allowed to return, not to the Land but YHVH the ELOHIM of their fathers.

> Yet the number of the sons of Israel will be like the sand of the sea, which cannot be measured or numbered; and in the place where it is said to them, "You are not My people," It will be said to them, "You are the sons of the living God." And the sons of Judah and the sons of Israel will be gathered together, and they will appoint for themselves one leader, (Messiah Yeshua, the Jewish Messiah) and they will go up from the land, (obviously not all the descendants of Ephraim can live in the Land of Israel as these are numerous and vast nations! But they can come to visit as tourists. For great will be the day of Jezreel.
>
> — Hosea 1:10-11

Their return would not be as Israelites or Ephraimites but as Gentile Nations.

Israelite blood has always been mixed among the nations because of the exile and also because of the extensive slave trade. Many conquering empires such as Greece and Rome traded in large quantities of Jewish slaves and even as early as the Phoenicians and Philistines sold Jewish and Israelite slaves.

In fact, Joseph, Ephraim and Manasseh's father was sold as a slave by his brothers to the Ishmaelites.

The House of Israel, the Northern Kingdom would be cut off forever and can never claim "Israelite rights."

> Then she conceived again and gave birth to a daughter. And YHVH said to him, "Name her Lo-ruhamah, for I will no longer have compassion on the house of Israel, that I would ever forgive them. But I will have compassion on the house of Judah and deliver them by the Lord their God, and will not deliver them by bow, sword, battle, horses or horsemen." When she had weaned Lo-ruhamah, she conceived and gave birth to a son. And the Lord said, "Name him Lo-ammi, for you are not My people and I am not your God."
> — Hosea 1:7-9

However, the promise to Ephraim is fulfilled in the fullness of the Gentiles that come into the Kingdom; these are the *Sheep Nations*.

> "When the Most High gave the nations their inheritance, When He separated the sons of man, He set the boundaries of the peoples According to the number of the sons of Israel.
> — Deuteronomy 32:8

The blood of Israel is mixed all over the world right now and is untraceable as it is so mixed just like salt is unrecognizable when mixed in a stew. However, with the advance of DNA and ancestry research, many people will show up as partly Jewish or partly Israelite mixed with many other ethnicities.

If I discover through ancestry research that I have 5% or 15% Japanese would that give me the rights to a Japanese passport? Of course not!

In the same way, Gentile believers in Messiah that have rediscovered the Hebrew Roots of the faith cannot claim Israelite identity or rights to the Land of Israel (like the Jews have). Both Jews and Gentiles receive salvation by grace through faith when they put their trust in the Jewish Messiah Yeshua; they become the One New Man.

> **For He Himself is our peace, who made both groups into one and broke down the barrier of the dividing wall, By abolishing in His flesh the enmity, which is the Law of commandments contained in (sacrificial) ordinances, so that in Himself (by becoming the Ultimate Sacrifice) He might make the two into one new man, thus establishing peace.**
>
> **– Ephesians 2:14-16**

But Jews will forever represent the Land of Israel and the nation of Israel, when Gentile believers will represent the nation they come from.

> **... for I will no longer have compassion on the house of Israel, that I would ever forgive them. But I will have compassion on the house of Judah and deliver them by the L<small>ORD</small> their God, and will not deliver them by bow, sword, battle, horses or horsemen."**
>
> **– Hosea 1:6-7**

THE NORTHERN KINGDOM IS REPRESENTED WITHIN THE JEWISH NATION OF TODAY

When the House of Israel, the Northern Kingdom (also called many times Ephraim) was exiled to Assyria, it ceased to exist as the House of Israel. It would never return from exile. When Yeshua came on the scene about 800 years later, the ones in the Land were the Jewish people. The Jewish people are initially the House of Judah or the Southern Kingdom with Jerusalem and the Temple Worship at its center. Together with Judah was always the tribe of Benjamin as Jerusalem is partly in the confines of Benjamin and partly on the confines of Judah. Most Levitical Priests and Aaron's line would be in the Holy City serving in the Temple.

When the House of Israel was being conquered by the Assyrians, many from the other ten tribes of the North relocated to the South and joined the House of Judah, losing their tribal identity and becoming Jews. The Jews that are living today in the Land carry within them the ancestry of some of the tribes of the North, and they are a prophetic fulfillment of the restoration of both Judah and Ephraim according to many prophetic scriptures. In my own family, some of the family names are from the tribe of Judah, but one of my family names is *Israel*. Maybe from my maternal grandmother's side they came from the House of Israel. *The two sticks meaning Judah and Joseph are already One in the Land of Israel today.*

> ... say to them, 'Thus says the Lord God, "Behold, I will take the stick of Joseph, which is in the hand of Ephraim, and the tribes of Israel, his companions; and I will put them with it, with the stick of Judah,

and make them one stick, and they will be one in My hand."' The sticks on which you write will be in your hand before their eyes. Say to them, 'Thus says the Lord God, "Behold, I will take the sons of Israel from among the nations where they have gone, and I will gather them from every side and bring them into their own land; and I will make them one nation in the land, on the mountains of Israel; and one king will be king for all of them; and they will no longer be two nations and no longer be divided into two kingdoms."

— Ezekiel 37:19-22

This prophecy is already fulfilled in modern-day Israel. The nation is not divided into the Northern and Southern Kingdom anymore.

Some portions of the ten northern tribes have preserved their Israelite identity (not influenced by the Two-House doctrines). They have known from time immemorial that they are of Israel and they carry tribal traditions as such like the Bnei Menashe in India that have been allowed to make *Aliyah* by the Israeli authorities. There may be other groups that after research, will be regarded as a proven Israelite group, and they may be allowed to return. Thus biblical prophecy is continually being fulfilled.

MESSIANIC GENTILES AND THE LAND OF ISRAEL

Non-Jewish believers (the promise of the fullness of the Gentiles and potential Sheep Nations), will have a special connection to the Land of Israel, being the Land of the Messiah. So we see that the Land of Israel is likened to the spiritual home of the millions of Messianic non-Jewish believers from the nations – in the same way that Rome is the spiritual home of most Christians (and especially the Catholics). Obviously not all these Catholics throughout the nations can claim rights to be a citizen of Rome. The same could be said about all of the descendants of the Spanish conquests in the Americas. Can you imagine if all these descendants would claim rights to Spain?

I believe that all believers from the nations are called to make *Spiritual Aliyah* – which is a "spiritual ascension" to Yah's (God's) Holy Land: As Sons and Daughters of the Father in heaven through the Jewish Messiah. *This is not to usurp the place of the Jews in their Land but to honor the God of Israel and the modern-day People of Israel by their presence.* They are also called to come and learn the ways of YHVH in His Land and to entreat His favor.

> Thus says the LORD of hosts, 'It will yet be that peoples will come, even the inhabitants of many cities. The inhabitants of one will go to another, saying, "Let us go at once to entreat the favor of YHVH, and to seek the LORD of hosts; I will also go." So many peoples and mighty nations will come to seek the LORD of hosts in Jerusalem and to entreat the favor of YHVH.' Thus says the LORD of hosts, 'In those days ten men from all the nations will grasp the hem of a garment of a Jew, saying, "Let us go with you, for we have heard that ELOHIM is with you."'
> — Zechariah 8:20-23

But notice that these Gentiles are called to *"grasp the hem of a garment of a Jew"* when they come to the Land. That speaks of letting yourself be guided by Israeli Jewish believers that have *Tsitsit* (the hem of the garment representing obedience to Yah's Torah instructions: See Numbers 15). These are not Orthodox Jews but Messianic Jews that can teach the nations Torah *without religion*! Instead, they teach with the presence and anointing of the Holy Spirit. *("ELOHIM is with you"* means His presence, power and anointing are implied!)

> Now it will come about that in the last days the mountain of the house of YHVH will be established as the chief of the mountains, and will be raised above the hills; and all the nations will stream to it. And many peoples will come and say, "Come, let us go up to the mountain of YHVH, to the house of the God of Jacob; That He may teach us concerning His ways and that we may walk in His paths." For the TORAH will go forth from Zion and the word of YHVH from Jerusalem.
> — Isaiah 2:2-3 (see also Zechariah 8 and Zechariah 14:16)

THE JEWISH REMNANT

Because of the slave trade (as early as the time of the Phoenicians and the Philistines, ancient Greece and Rome, then the Muslim and Christian nations) many Israelites and Judeans were mixed within other nations and lost their identity. *This world is indeed a mixed world*: Nearly no one has "pure blood" of this or of that ethnic group—especially in the Western world, including Europe and the Americas.

However, the God of Israel has kept for Himself *a remnant of recognizable Jews* that did not forfeit their identity, in spite of severe persecutions while in exile. It is these Jews that He began to awaken by the end of the 19th Century to return home after 2,000 years of exile, when the Zionist Movement was born. This birth was the fulfillment of numerous prophecies in the Bible (see Ezekiel 36:24-28; Ezekiel 37; Isaiah 49; Jeremiah 31; 32:36-44; Amos 9:11-15; Psalm 105:8-11).

The following scriptures can describe the Zionist Movement, its impact on the returning exiled Jews, and its influence on the nations.

> A Song of Ascents. When ADONAI restored the captives of Zion, it was as if we were dreaming. Then our mouth was filled with laughter, and our tongue with a song of joy. Then they said among the nations, "ADONAI has done great things for them." ADONAI has done great things for us —we are joyful!
>
> — Psalm 126:1-3

THE SEPHARDIC JEWS

Among the Jews that were expelled out of Spain by the Spanish Inquisition, the ancestry is more apparent, as the Jews were in Spain since the time of King Solomon and they did not intermarry (for the most part). Persecutions kept them separate. Their choice was not to convert but to be expelled, resulting in their losing everything. They did this in 1492 at the official break out of the Catholic Spanish Inquisition.

THE CONVERSO JEWS

Among those Jews that converted to Catholicism, mostly under force and cruelty, (becoming known as Converso Jews) some of them married among their Converso brethren to preserve their Judaism. Many or most of those called New Christians were so shunned that they were not permitted to marry any "Old Christians" – consequently, they had to marry another Converso Jew.

Eventually many or most may have intermarried with non-Jews and were lost to the nation of Israel altogether *until recently*. Many of the Converso Jews are waking up to their identity as Jews *500 years* after the Spanish Inquisition started. Inquisition archives with their family names listed have been found; the Spanish authorities are even issuing a Spanish passport to anyone that can prove some Spanish Jewish ancestry. Most of those who converted and their descendants (about 60 million of them) are not aware of their Jewish ancestry, even though many of them carry peculiar traditions and language idioms from the Jewish-Spanish *Ladino* language. This is an unstoppable movement of restoration, fulfilling numerous prophecies – especially the following:

> **The exiles of this army of Bnei-Yisrael will possess what belonged to the Canaanites as far as Zarephath, while the exiles of Jerusalem, who are in Sepharad, will possess the cities of the Negev.**
>
> **– Obadiah 20**

Sepharad is Spain. I believe that many of these groups will return to their identity as Jews: *Anusim* (forced ones), *Marranos* ('pigs' in Spanish, named as such by the Catholics), Crypto-Jews (they kept their Jewish identity underground), and Converso Jews. They *will* recognize the Jewish Messiah instead of the Catholic-Greek Jesus Christ, and a chosen remnant will even make *Aliyah* (return to the Land of their ancestors) to settle the Negev Desert. This process is already in motion, and we will hear more about this in due time.

However, the only ones that still kept longing for the Land of Israel were those Jews that did *not* convert. They were all throughout Europe and the Balkans, and they kept close contact with the Land of Israel, often supporting the Jewish community in the Old City. Even during the most terrible of conquests there were Jews that remained in the Land.

Those Jews that remained Jews in spite of inquisition, pogroms, crusades and the *Shoah* (Nazi Holocaust), are the ones that YHVH awakened to bring to the Land and to establish the modern state of Israel on May 14, 1948.

Will these Jews respond to a Christian gospel? For the most part, *no*. We were persecuted by Christianity and remained Jews in spite of all opposition.

THE UNITED NATIONS FOR ISRAEL

The goal of the Messianic Apostolic Prophetic (MAP) Movement was the establishment of *The United Nations for Israel*.

Ruth-like Messianic Nations are being born: Those that will stand unconditionally with Israel until her full restoration to the whole Land of Promise and her *ELOHIM*. Not because the citizens of these Ruth Nations will all move *en masse* to Israel (it would be impossible) or because they would try "to convert the Jews" but because they "would be with her" in the international and political arena and the spirit. They would support her *unconditionally*.

> But Ruth said, "Do not urge me to leave you or turn back from following you; for where you go, I will go, and where you lodge, I will lodge. Your people shall be my people, and your God, my God. Where

you die, I will die, and there I will be buried. Thus may YHVH do to me, and worse, if anything but death parts you and me.

— Ruth 1:16-17

These Ruth-like nations would not hide the Jewish Messiah. They would let Him shine in all His Jewishness and full glory, through Shabbats, Feasts and Biblical celebrations, Messianic praise, worship, holiness, righteousness, and unconditional love to Israel (like Ruth to Naomi). They would keep their national identity and all that is Godly and holy in their cultures – and they would join the Jewish believers in their Olive Tree, thus becoming grafted-in believers. Each one of these grafted-in believers could start standing in the gap for the turning of their nations from goat nations to Sheep Nations by espousing and implementing *Biblical Politics:*

1. In their internal affairs by adhering to the social and moral instructions in the Bible including the Torah and the 10 Commandments: The sanctity of life; the sanctity of creational gender marriages of a male with a female; social justice to the poor, the widow, the orphan and the weak, etc.
2. In their Foreign Policy Affairs that would be favorable to Israel and to Yah's Land Covenant with Abraham, Isaac and Jacob until 1,000 generations.
3. By not joining the Globalist takeover of the "new world order" but remaining faithful to the God of Israel and trusting Him above all.

UNIFY IS HERE TO STAY AND TO PREPARE THE WAY FOR THE RETURN OF MESSIAH TO YERUSHALAYIM.

> "Many nations will join themselves to YHVH in that day and will become My people. Then I will dwell in your midst, and you will know that the Lord of hosts has sent Me to you. YHVH will possess Judah as His portion in the holy land, and will again choose Jerusalem. 'Be silent, all flesh, before YHVH; for He is aroused from His holy habitation."
> — Zechariah 2:11-13*

Turning nations into Sheep Nations, one person at a time, will cause YHVH to *"possess Judah as His portion."* He will reveal Himself to His people through the Ruth-like character of these Sheep Nations and individuals.

This revelation would be achieved by:

- Comprehensive reeducation: Using T.V. programs; Israel Tours; and fighting for Israel in every arena.
- Changing the heart of Church and governments from the devastating religious system of Replacement Theology Christianity to the Gospel made in Zion – from the Greek Jesus Christ to the Jewish Messiah Yeshua.
- Displaying the power of His Kingdom through love and holiness – followed by signs, wonders, and miracles!
- Recovering the Gospel made in Zion that the Jewish apostles preached 2,000 years ago and bring that Gospel to the nations.

---

* Verses 13-15 in some translations.

UNIFY IS HOUSING THE THIRD DAY REVIVAL

Once again we say: The Revival of the Third Day calls us to return to *Him*, to Yeshua the Jewish Messiah and to the love and *honor* of the Jewish people—the Israel of *today*, who is the Mother of the Nations. Yeshua is calling us to lay down our weapons, our lies and arrogance, to lay down all strife and seek *Him*. Only *He* can restore us as we *repent* from all personal sins and doctrinal lies. We *must seek him* and become what we are called to be: *United Nations for Israel* housing the Third Day Revival!

CHAPTER 8

THE RULE OF MESSIAH ON EARTH
THE PLAN FOR THE NATIONS IN THIS NEW JUBILEE CYCLE

> All this energy issues from Messiah: E<small>LOHIM</small> raised him from death and set him on a throne in deep heaven, in charge of running the universe, everything from galaxies to governments, no name and no power exempt from his rule. And not just for the time being, but forever. He is in charge of it all, has the final word on everything. At the center of all this, Messiah rules the Ecclesia. The ecclesia, you see, is not peripheral to the world; the world is peripheral to the ecclesia. The ecclesia is Messiah's body, in which he speaks and acts, by which he fills everything with his presence.
>
> — *Ephesians 1:20-23 MSG*

---

*T*HREE SIGNIFICANT EVENTS were converging in 2017, the Biblical year 5777/5778:

1. The Jubilee of the unification of Jerusalem after the miracle Six-Day War on June 1967
2. The 120th Year of the establishing of the first Zionist Congress in Basel in August of 1897
3. The 500th year since Luther's Reformation on 1517 Halloween (or All Saints Day October 31st)

YHVH spoke to me as we started the new *Yovel* (Jubilee) Cycle the following:

I am the Ruler of the Nations, and I am looking for vessels of Glory that will implement my absolute sovereignty and rulership on planet earth. The Nations are My inheritance and all the ends of the earth My possession. I am knocking on the Gates of Nations to come in as the King of Glory and to overthrow wicked, unrighteous governments and establish righteous governments. I am looking to see Sheep Nations come forth! What seems impossible with humans is possible with YHVH. My Bride will implement this, My will, for the nations.

SHEEP NATIONS

In 2001 I was visited by Yeshua on Christmas day while visiting my native land Chile, from which I made *aliyah,* or returned to my ancient homeland Israel as promised in the Holy Scriptures. I was in prayer that day while most churches were in services celebrating the pagan date that was established in the 4th Century as the birth date of Messiah. I was in prayer that day, and Yeshua showed up and asked me a question: "How many nations will be Sheep Nations if I returned *today?*" He then proceeded to tell me that He will judge the nations according to these two principles:

1. How have the nations behaved with His people Israel (the Jewish people)?
2. How are the nations honoring His Ten Commandments or His Torah?

I knew in 2001 that no nation qualified as a Sheep Nation, so I begged Yeshua for *more time* to run with the message of Sheep Nations and of repentance towards YHVH! It was to the Church we needed to run, and we have run into 50 nations and counting. Our books, E-Books, music CD's, Shabbat letters, teachings, T.V. programs, Bible School, and tours of Israel have run together with us multiplying the *seed* of His Word and this calling to:

WORLDWIDE REPENTANCE FOR A WORLDWIDE AWAKENING

By His grace and faithfulness to carry us through and by the devotion of our precious partners and disciples we have broken through the impossible territory, and now it is time to *take possession of land and nations with the Gospel made in Zion.*

THE ARISING OF HIS BRIDE WILL POSITION NEW GOVERNMENTS

We are destined to be a catalyst for the establishment of righteous governments on the earth. While most Christians are passively waiting for a takeover by the New World Order and the Antichrist, His *true Bride* is *actively* working for a *takeover* of righteous presidents and righteous governments:

> Now therefore, O kings, show discernment; take warning, O judges of the earth. Worship YHVH with reverence and rejoice with trembling.
>
> — Psalm 2:10-11

The nations belong to Yeshua, not to the devil. The nations are His inheritance—but a lukewarm, immoral, idolatrous, deceived church, full of Replacement Theology and pagan Christmas and Easter traditions, fed with a sugar-coated gospel has not had the strength, glory, power or authority to implement His will on earth! It is through His Body comprised of Jew and Gentile, grafted into the Olive Tree (not the Christmas tree) that He works His will on earth. Since the divorce of the Church from its Jewish roots and foundations by Constantine and the Council of Nicaea in the 4th Century the nations have been further and further away from becoming *Sheep Nations*. The Bride of Messiah has been undone or in hiding. But in this New Jubilee Cycle it is *time* for the anointed and Holy Messianic Apostolic Prophetic Bride in combat boots to *arise*!

He is knocking on the *gates* of *nations* to position *righteous governments*, and He can implement that only as His Bride goes into both *prayer* and *action* in *every* arena, including *financial* and the "political" which I will call *governmental*.

> At the center of all this, Messiah rules the Ecclesia. The ecclesia, you see, is not peripheral to the world; the world is peripheral to the ecclesia. The ecclesia is Messiah's body, in which he speaks and acts, by which he fills everything with his presence.
>
> — Ephesians 1:20-23 MSG

PREPARED TO RULE AND REIGN

> To the intent that now the manifold wisdom of God might be made known by the church to the principalities and powers in the heavenly places.
>
> — Ephesians 3:10 NKJV

A radical change of mind is happening in His true Bride in combat boots. The Bride is being cleansed from the ravages of religion and most particularly Babylonian Christianity, pagan feasts and alienation from Israel and the Torah. This change is preparing us to marry the Jewish King, but it is also preparing us to *rule* and *reign* with Him and to *implement His reign on earth*.

WHAT RELIGION HAS MASKED

> Elohim raised him from death and set him on a throne in deep heaven, in charge of running the universe, everything from galaxies to governments, no name and no power exempt from his rule.
>
> — Ephesians 1:21 MSG

Religion has masked the fact that *Messiah rules in this world* and not only in the world to come. Interestingly enough, the very mistaken and cruel Crusaders knew it and were trying to implement His rule on the earth by conquering Jerusalem on the 11th Century and burning alive the Jewish population there while singing praise hymns! They were sorely mistaken as His kingdom must be implemented by His Spirit and in His order. And His order is as usual:

TO THE JEW FIRST

By getting rid of the Jews, the Crusaders were getting further away from bringing His rule on earth: They were actually going opposite. Christianity through the Crusaders was bringing on the New World Order with Jerusalem at its center already in the 11th Century A.D.! They were fulfilling the desire of the builders of the Tower of Babel in Genesis 11:

"*Let us build for ourselves a tower to reach heaven. Let us make for ourselves a name so we will not be scattered...*"

The Christian crusaders were defeated by the Muslims. Christians are again being defeated by the Muslims in the 21st Century! ISIS is advancing in what used to be Christian nations all over Europe, America, and South America. History is repeating itself ten centuries later! (note: This takeover is because Christianity is divorced from the pure Hebrew foundations of the faith. Once we see Christians repent from Replacement Theology, we will see a *massive* take-back.)

10 JUBILEES SINCE LUTHER'S REFORMATION

The year of 2017 commemorated and completed 10 Jubilees, namely 500 years since the start of Martin Luther's Reformation. It is quite revealing that this reformation started officially in Halloween which is adopted by Christianity as All Saints Day. However, Halloween is *All Witches Day,* and it is far from being a holy day or celebration. That was the imperfection of Luther's Reformation, though it touched on the important issue of salvation by grace through faith, it failed to reconnect to the Jewish roots and the original Gospel made in Zion, and it left the Church hanging in the balance.

10 IS THE NUMBER OF COMPLETION, ORDER, AND JUDGMENT

YHVH is judging *all* religion and religious systems and establishing His Kingdom through His Bride, wanting to get His inheritance, the nation's back. He wants Sheep Nations. He wants righteous governments; He wants a *takeover* of righteousness! At the darkest time, He wants His glory to shine. *Nothing is impossible with Him*:

> "Arise, shine; for your light has come, and the glory of the Lord has risen upon you. "For behold, darkness will cover the earth and deep darkness the peoples; but the Lord will rise upon you and His glory will appear upon you. "Nations will come to your light, and kings to the brightness of your rising.
>
> — Isaiah 60:1-3

This scripture is about Israel being the Chief Sheep Nation but is also applicable for *His Bride that has repented from Replacement Theology, going past Luther's reformation and has returned home to the original Gospel made in Zion: Joining Israel rather than Replacing Israel.*

ISRAEL THE CHIEF SHEEP NATION AND THE JUBILEE OF YERUSHALAYIM

The real name of Jerusalem is *Yerushalayim*, which includes the Hebrew words *yerusha* and *shalom*. *Yerusha* means "inheritance." *Shalayim* means "a double portion of shalom or completeness and wellbeing."

2017 marked 50 years since the miracle Six-Day War when the Holy City was finally *unified*. It will be good once and for all to understand that the territory that Israel gained in this miracle war is a Covenant Issue and was given to her by YHVH Himself. Any nation that is trying to make her go back to the borders before 1967 or 1948 will find itself in serious trouble!

> On that day I will make Jerusalem a heavy stone for all the people. All who lift it will be hurt. And all the nations of the earth will be gathered against it.
>
> — Zechariah 12:3 NKJV

All the End-time scriptures indicate that Israel is the most critical nation in the world *and Yerushalayim* (Jerusalem) *the center of the world*. A failure to understand this will cause untold woes. She is not the most important because of her decision but because of Yah's (God's) Choice. She is YHVH's inheritance, and thus *all* the nations are called to come up to Zion in these End-times. Rain and blessing in the nations will depend on this – that world governments will honor Israel and the King of Israel who is *Yeshua*!

> Then it will come about that any who are left of all the nations that went against Jerusalem will go up from year to year to worship the King, The LORD of Hosts and to celebrate the Feast of Booths. And it will be that whichever of the families of the earth does not go up to Jerusalem to worship the King, the LORD of hosts, there will be no rain on them.
>
> — Zechariah 14:16-17

ISRAEL IS BEING PREPARED

An awakening is taking place in Israel, there is a miraculous turning towards a restoration of identity, and we will see more of this in the days to come as two particular groups begin to gain momentum: The Messianic Jews and the Religious Orthodox Zionists. They will seem to run parallel for a while, but it will culminate in an all-encompassing *revival* in Israel:

> I will pour out on the house of David and on the inhabitants of Jerusalem, the Spirit of grace and of supplication, so that they will look on Me whom they have pierced; and they will mourn for Him, as one mourns for an only son, and they will weep bitterly over Him like the bitter weeping over a firstborn.
> — Zechariah 12:10

A UNITED NATIONS FOR ISRAEL IS BEING PREPARED!

I will elaborate more on this in the days to come as it is the new thrust of all our Israel tours and many of our actions in the nations. Theodor Herzl, the Jewish Prophet that believed for Israel to become a nation again and established the first Zionist Congress in 1897 said:

"*Im tirzu ein zo hagadah!*" Which means: "*If you will it this will not be a fable!*"

Can nations *unite* for Israel as much as the obsolete, irrelevant, new world order United Nations today is staunchly against Israel? Yes, they can, but there will be a *new prophetic platform* for this to happen with *authority from heaven*.

> "Many nations will join themselves to YHVH in that day and will become My people. Then I will dwell in your midst, and you will know

that the L ORD of hosts has sent Me to you. YHVH will possess Judah as His portion in the holy land, and will again choose Jerusalem.

— Zechariah 2:11-12

And to the opinionated "politically, or humanistic 'correct'" He says: "*Shut up!*"

Be silent, all flesh, before YHVH; for He is aroused from His holy habitation."

— Zechariah 2:13

Bride of Messiah, *put your combat boots on* and take ground in the ministry, in the Harvest Field, in the financial arena, in the market-place, in the Governmental (political) arena. Do not put any limitations on how the King desires to use us to implement His sovereign rule on the earth. It is the Messiah, *not* the Anti-messiah that is *ruling*.

CHAPTER 9

THE TRICK... OR THE TREE?
A CHRISTMAS MESSAGE

He who has an ear, let him hear what the Spirit says to the churches. To him who overcomes I will give to eat from the tree of life, which is in the midst of the Paradise of God.

— *Revelation 2:7*

---

*A*S WE ENTER into the Christmas Season, it is essential to revisit some facts about Christmas. First of all, a disclaimer: We believe the Messiah's birth to be the most critical event in the history of the universe! If He had not been born, he would not have been able to pay the price for our sins, and each one of us would be under judgment. However, the time has come to put His birth in its original context. So, leaving all emotions and feelings aside, let us talk *facts*.

> She is a tree of life to those who take hold of her, and happy are all who hold her fast.
>
> — Proverbs 3:18

THE TREE OF LIFE

There were two principal trees in the Garden of Eden. One was the Tree of Life, and one was the Tree of Knowledge of Good and Evil (Genesis 2:17). I call the Tree of Knowledge, the "Tree of Death" as eating from that tree brought death to all humanity. Yeshua said, "I am the Way, the Truth, and the Life." King David said: "Your Torah is Life." King Solomon described wisdom derived from the Torah of YHVH as a Tree of Life, and the beginning of Wisdom is the Fear of YHVH.

> The fear of YHVH is the beginning of wisdom; a good understanding have all those who do His commandments; His praise endures forever.
>
> — Psalm 111:10

Yeshua is the Living Torah as He is the Word made flesh (John 1:14)! The Torah, *Pentateuch*, or the Five Books of Moses is the blueprint and foundation of the entire Bible. Yeshua is the Torah made flesh (Matthew 5:17-21), He is the Tree of Life. In that context, would you say that Christmas is from the Tree of Life or the Tree of Knowledge, the "Tree of Death?" What is the most prominent symbol of Christmas?

THE CHRISTMAS TREE

How It All Got Started

Long before the advent of Christianity, plants and trees that remained green all year had a special meaning for people in the winter. Just as people today decorate their homes during the festive season with pine, spruce, and fir trees, ancient peoples hung evergreen boughs over their doors and windows. In many countries it was believed that evergreens would keep away witches, ghosts, evil spirits, and illness.

Did You Know?

Christmas trees are grown in all 50 states of the USA including Hawaii and Alaska.

In the Northern hemisphere, the shortest day and longest night of the year falls on December 21 or December 22 and is called the winter solstice. Many ancient people believed that the sun was a god and that winter came every year because the sun god had become sick and weak. They celebrated the solstice because it meant that at last the sun god would begin to get well. Evergreen boughs reminded them of all the green plants that would grow again when the sun god was strong and summer would return.

The ancient Egyptians worshiped a god called Ra, who had the head of a hawk and wore the sun as a blazing disk in his crown. At the solstice, when Ra began to recover from the illness, the Egyptians filled their homes with green palm rushes which symbolized for them the triumph of life over death.

Early Romans marked the solstice with a feast called the Saturnalia in honor of Saturn, the god of agriculture. The Romans knew that the solstice meant that soon farms and orchards would be green and fruitful. To mark the occasion, they decorated their homes and temples with evergreen boughs. In Northern Europe the mysterious Druids, the priests of the ancient Celts, also decorated their temples with evergreen boughs as a symbol of everlasting life. The fierce Vikings in Scandinavia thought that evergreens were the special plant of the sun god, Balder.

Germany is credited with starting the Christmas tree tradition as we now know it in the 16th Century when devout Christians brought decorated trees into their homes. Some built Christmas pyramids of wood and decorated them with evergreens and candles if wood was scarce. (History.com Editors)

We have found it in Japan, in Ecuador, in Africa and even in Israel, decorated and full of silver, gold, and lights. People who do not know Yeshua (Jesus), neither are they interested in Him or the Gospel, *love* Christmas because of the decorations. Do they get saved because of it? No! However, they love it. But what does the Bible say about decorating trees as a religious act?

Hear the word which the Lord speaks to you, O house of Israel. Thus says the Lord, "Do not learn the way of the nations, and do not be terrified by the signs of the heavens although the nations are terrified by them; For the customs of the peoples are delusion; because it is wood cut from the forest, the work of the hands of a craftsman with a cutting tool. "They decorate it with silver and with gold; they fasten it with nails and with hammers so that it will not totter.

— Jeremiah 10:1-4

The Holy Scriptures strictly forbids the decorating of trees as emblems of worship as this is a pagan custom and YHVH is *Holy:*

Blessed are those who do His commandments, that they may have the right to the tree of life, and may enter through the gates into the city.

— Revelation 22:14 NKJV

Could it be that we need to give up pagan traditions like the putting up of Christmas trees so we can have the right to the Tree of Life?

Is it wise to keep on mixing emblems of pagan worship into our celebrations? The Prophet Hosea warns us that it can affect our children and all our generations:

My people are destroyed for lack of knowledge. Because you have rejected knowledge, also I will reject you from being priest for Me;

> Because you have forgotten the law of your God, I also will forget your children.
>
> — Hosea 4:6 NKJV

Have we forgotten the Law-Torah of our God? Have we made the Word of ELOHIM (God) null by our traditions?

> And He answered and said to them, "Why do you yourselves transgress the commandment of God for the sake of your tradition?
>
> — Matthew 15:3

PROTESTANTS BANNED CHRISTMAS

From the 16th Century the Protestant Reformation banned Christmas as a pagan celebration. In America it was forbidden in some areas until 1870.

"Shocking as it sounds, followers of Jesus Christ in both America and England helped pass laws making it illegal to observe Christmas, believing it was an insult to God to honor a day associated with ancient paganism," according to "Shocked by the Bible" (Thomas Nelson Inc, 2008). "Most Americans today are unaware that Christmas was banned in Boston from 1659 to 1681."

All Christmas activities, including dancing, seasonal plays, games, singing carols, cheerful celebration and especially drinking were banned by the Puritan-dominated Parliament of England in 1644, with the Puritans of New England following suit. Christmas was outlawed in Boston, and the Plymouth colony made celebrating Christmas a criminal offense, according to "Once Upon a Gospel".

Christmas trees and decorations were considered to be unholy pagan rituals, and the Puritans also banned traditional Christmas foods such as mince pies and pudding. Puritan laws required that stores and businesses remain open all day on Christmas, and town criers walked through the streets on Christmas Eve calling out "No Christmas, no Christmas!" (Melina, Livescience.com)

It is not a secret that Christmas is pagan, that it is not Messiah's date of birth, that the traditions are pagan – so why are those who consider themselves believers and disciples of Messiah still celebrating it? And why are they still putting Christmas trees in their home and churches? *Why keep on marketing and propagating a lie?*

Are believers in the Messiah from the nations to be attached to the Christmas Tree or to the Olive Tree which represents the Nation of Israel and the Torah given to Israel, starting with the Ten Commandments?

> **But if some of the branches were broken off, and you, being a wild olive, were grafted in among them and became partaker with them of the rich root of the olive tree, do not be arrogant toward the branches; but if you are arrogant, remember that it is not you who supports the root, but the root supports you.**
>
> **— Romans 11:17-18**

Does the *rich root* of the Olive Tree, which is the Torah, condone the putting up and decorating of trees as acts of worship? I believe I have amply proven that this is an act of pagan worship, even if you mean well. This is what it means in the spiritual realm, and it carries consequences just like the eating of the Tree of Knowledge carried consequences for Adam and all of humanity. Trees "speak" in the spiritual realm and the Christmas Tree speaks of pagan worship. Whether we like it or not, whether we mean it or not – putting up a Christmas Tree in your home, public place or Church is putting up an idol on the altar. It is certainly not a source of blessing as beautiful as it may be.

> **A good tree cannot bear bad fruit, nor can a bad tree bear good fruit. Every tree that does not bear good fruit is cut down and thrown into the fire.**
>
> **— Matthew 7: 18-19**

Are we to love a pagan tradition more than God's Word?

THE BIRTH OF MESSIAH

His place of birth: Beth-Lechem Judea, Israel.

> **But as for you, Bethlehem Ephrathah, too little to be among the clans of Judah, from you One will go forth for Me to be ruler in Israel. His goings forth are from long ago, from the days of eternity.**
>
> **— Micah 5:2**

His earthly lineage: Jewish, the Tribe of Judah from the House of David (see Matthew 1 for the genealogy of Messiah).

> And one of the elders said to me, "Stop weeping; behold, the Lion that is from the tribe of Judah, the Root of David, has overcome so as to open the book and its seven seals."
>
> — Revelation 5:5

His heavenly lineage – YHVH the Father in heaven.

> The angel answered and said to her, "The Holy Spirit will come upon you, and the power of the Most High will overshadow you; and for that reason the holy Child shall be called the Son of God."
>
> — Luke 1:35

His birth name: Yeshua, meaning "Salvation."
Take into consideration that the angel did not speak Greek or English to Joseph, but he spoke Hebrew. He called the boy by the name the God of Israel, His Father gave Him, and it was not Jesus or *Ieso* but Yeshua. Yeshua means "*salvation*." Jesus is not the original name but a transliteration.

> She will bear a Son; and you shall call His name Yeshua, for He will save His people from their sins.
>
> — Matthew 1:21

His time of birth: Some scholars believe it was during Sukkot – the Feast of Tabernacles and other scholars believe it was on Rosh Chodesh, the First Day of the First Month (*Nissan*) leading to Passover on the 14th day of the first month. Most scholars agree that He was not born in the winter or on December 25th. They calculate the date according to the Priestly Courses that fitted the Order of Abijah, according to Zechariah, the father of Yochanan the Immerser (John the Baptizer). Also, according to the visitation of the Angel Gabriel to Miriam (Mary) on the sixth month of Elisheva's (Elizabeth) pregnancy.

> **In the days of Herod, king of Judea, there was a priest named Zacharias, of the division of Abijah; and he had a wife from the daughters of Aaron, and her name was Elizabeth.**
> — Luke 1:5

> **Then in the sixth month the angel Gabriel was sent from ADONAI to a city in Galilee called Natzeret, to a virgin engaged to a man whose name was Joseph, of the house of David; and the virgin's name was Miriam.**
> — Luke 1:26-27

Celebration of Yeshua's birth-traditions: There was praise and joy.

> **And suddenly there appeared with the angel a multitude of the heavenly host praising God and saying, "Glory to God in the highest, and on earth peace among men with whom He is pleased."**
> — Luke 2:13-14

Brit Milah – Covenant of Circumcision on the 8th day.

> **And when eight days had passed, before His circumcision, His name was then called Yeshua, the name given by the angel before He was conceived in the womb.**
> — Luke 2:21

Presentation at the Holy Temple in Jerusalem, 40 days after His birth.

> And when the days for their purification according to the Torah of Moses were completed, they brought Him up to Jerusalem to present Him to Adonai.
>
> — Luke 2:22

Worship: Foreigners from the East come to worship the King of the Jews.

> After coming into the house they saw the Child with Miriam (Mary) His mother; and they fell to the ground and worshiped Him. Then, opening their treasures, they presented to Him gifts of gold, frankincense, and myrrh.
>
> — Matthew 2:11

It is clear from the Holy Scriptures that the Savior, the Messiah, is Jewish from the Tribe of Judah, from the House of David born in Israel. It is also clear that His name means "*salvation*," that He is Divine yet born in the flesh as a Jew and that His time of birth does not match the traditional time of Christmas on December 25th. It is also clear that the traditions surrounding His birth are very different than the traditions of Christmas.

THE BIRTH OF CHRISTMAS

Ancestral worship:

Early Christians wanted to convert pagans. . . but they were also fascinated by their traditions. "Christians of that period are quite interested in paganism," he said. "It's obviously something they think is a bad thing, but it's also something they think is worth remembering. It's what their ancestors did." (Pappas)

- Christmas' place of birth: Eastern Rome – Byzantium

The first recorded date of Christmas being celebrated on December 25th was in 336 A.D., during the time of the Roman Emperor Constantine (he was the first Christian Roman Emperor). (Whychristmas.com)

A few years later, Pope Julius I officially declared that the birth of Jesus would be celebrated on the 25th December.

- Christmas' earthly lineage: Roman Emperor Constantine.
- Christmas' spiritual lineage: Sun Worship – The winter witchcraft solstice, *Saturnalia,* the "Day of the Unconquered Sun": December 25th might have also been chosen because the Winter Solstice and the ancient pagan Roman midwinter festivals called Saturnalia and *Dies Natalis Solis Invict* (The Day of Birth of the Unconquered Sun or the pagan god Jupiter-Baal-Zeus-Tamuz) took place in December around this date-so it was time when people already celebrated things. (Nazarenesoftheworld.info)
- It's time of birth: Christmas was adopted in year 336 A.D. after the signing and establishing of the Council of Nicaea where Roman Emperor Constantine called for a complete divorce from the Jews and everything Jewish.

At that time he established pagan celebrations for the Church to *replace* the Hebrew Biblical ones. This includes exchanging Shabbat for Sunday (the day that he worshiped the sun god); Passover for Easter (the day of celebration of the goddess *Ishtar* or *Semiramis*); and Christmas on the 25th of December, the shortest day of the year—the day of celebration to the "Birth of the Unconquered Sun" or *Tamuz*.

Below is an excerpt from the Council of Nicaea by Emperor Constantine 325 A.D.

> We ought not therefore to have anything in common with the Jew, for the Saviour has shown us another way; our worship following a more legitimate and more convenient course (the order of the days of the week: And consequently in unanimously adopting this mode, we desire, dearest brethren to separate ourselves from the detestable company of the Jew. (Percival)

Emperor Constantine set himself up to be the Pope of the Church that he established and Christianity, the religion of the Roman Empire, became totally divorced from its Scriptural-Biblical-Jewish and apostolic foundations.

Important to note: For 300 years or more the believers in Messiah did not celebrate Christmas. The Early Messianic Church in Jerusalem would have never agreed to it because of its pagan roots and traditions.

- Christmas' name: From Greek, "Christ-Mass."
- Origins of the Catholic Mass: The round wafer is a symbol of the sun. It is normally placed during ceremonial masses on a monstrance with a crescent moon, symbolizing the plunging of the sun into the womb of the goddess. Some monstrance bear the

letters "SFS," which represents 666, as S was the sixth letter in the ancient Greek alphabet and F is the sixth letter in our alphabet.

The round disc in the crescent moon was a symbol of ancient Babylon, and is found in all the ancient religions. In Catholic cathedrals, these symbols are very prominent, often depicting a round form of mother and child within the crescent moon.

The rebirth of the sun god was celebrated by the eating of round bread in Babylonian times, and was common in Mithraism and Osiris worship. Historian Alexander Hislop says this:

And here, in a so-called Christian Church, a brilliant plate of silver, "in the form of the SUN," is so placed on the altar, that everyone who adores at the altar must bow in lowly reverence before that image of the "SUN." Whence, I ask, could that have come, than from the ancient SUN-worship, or the worship of Baal? And when the wafer is placed so that the silver "SUN" is fronting the "round" wafer, whose "roundness" is so important an element in the Romish Mystery, is only another symbol of Baal, or the sun, what can be the meaning of it, but to show to those who have eyes to see that the "Wafer" itself is only another symbol of Baal. (Amazing Discoveries)

CHRISTMAS TRADITIONS

Now that we have established that Yeshua, the Jewish Messiah, and Christmas were not born in the same place, at the same time or from the same lineage, let us determine if the traditions of Christmas are holy and if they are sanctioned by YHVH, the Father.

There are so many traditions before and during the Christmas Season, and so I will touch on the most prominent ones.

TALES DISCONNECTED FROM TRUTH
Santa Claus:

> The author best known for creating the Headless Horseman also created the iconic image of Santa flying in a sleigh. In his 1819 series of short stories The Sketch Book of Geoffrey Crayon, New York native Washington Irving described a dream in which St. Nicholas soared across the sky in a weightless wagon. The stories became so popular, they spawned a Christmas revival of sorts in the States, and even Charles Dickens is said to have credited Irving's work for inspiring his classic holiday tale *A Christmas Carol*. (TIME.com)

Children are taught to "ask Santa for gifts or whatever they need." Lately, I have heard of movie clips that show Santa Clause praying for healing and healing the children. Beloved ones, this is *idolatry*. There is *one* mediator between Yah (God) and man, and *He* is not Santa Claus or the Virgin Mary!

The sin of idolatry causes a curse to fall upon the coming generations; to the third and fourth generation:

You shall have no other gods before Me. 'You shall not make for yourself a carved image—any likeness of anything that is in heaven above, or that is in the earth beneath, or that is in the water under the earth; you shall not bow down to them nor serve them. For I, the Lord your God, am a jealous God, visiting the iniquity of the fathers upon the children to the third and fourth generations of those who hate Me, but showing mercy to thousands, to those who love Me and keep My commandments.

– Deuteronomy 5:7-10

Gimmicks to promote alcohol and drinking during Christmas:

Nor thieves, nor covetous, nor drunkards, nor revilers, nor extortioners will inherit the kingdom of God.

– 1 Corinthians 6:10

Like the Energizer Bunny, Rudolph the Red-Nosed Reindeer got his start as an advertising gimmick. A copywriter named Robert L. May first created the merry misfit in 1939 to lure shoppers into the Montgomery Ward department store. Frosty the Snowman and his famous corncob pipe couldn't escape the clutches of the advertising industry either; a whiskey maker in 1890 used Frosty's likeness to showcase an entirely different kind of holiday cheer. Once Prohibition ended, the chain-smoking snowman quickly became the go-to guy for alcohol ads, appearing in posters for Miller beer, Jack Daniel's, Ballantine ale, Rheingold beer, Schlitz beer, Oretel's lager beer, Chivas Regal scotch, Fort Pitt pale ale, Mount Whitney beer and Four Roses. (TIME.com)

PAGAN PROMISCUITY - KISSING UNDER THE MISTLETOE

According to Celtic and Teutonic legend, mistletoe is magical — it can heal wounds, increase fertility, bring good luck, and ward off evil spirits. The tradition of kissing under the mistletoe didn't begin until the Victorian era, a surprising origin given the stuffy and sexually repressive behavior of the time. Actually, it's not very surprising at all. (TIME.com)

CHRISTMAS TREE WORSHIP

> Only acknowledge your iniquity, that you have transgressed against the YHVH your God, and hast scattered your ways to the strangers under every green tree, and you have not obeyed my voice, says the Lord.
>
> — Jeremiah 3:13

Even before the arrival of Christianity, *pagan* Romans and then Germans decorated evergreen trees to brighten the dark, gloomy days of the winter solstice. The first "Christmas trees" appeared in Strasbourg in the 17th Century and spread to Pennsylvania in the 1820s with the arrival of German immigrants. When Queen Victoria married Germany's Prince Albert in 1840, he brought the tradition to England. Eight years later, the first American newspaper ran a picture of the royal Christmas tree, and Americans outside Pennsylvania quickly followed suit. (TIME.com)

Long before the birth of the LORD Jesus Christ evergreens were used by the pagans in their superstitious worship. They took their ability to remain green year round as a symbol of immortality, fertility, and the resurrection of the sun god. In the northern regions of Europe they were brought inside also under the superstitious notion that the woodland spirits and fairies would live in them during the winter and thus survive the cold. (No doubt this would also give "good luck" to the people as well.) In Italy evergreens were used to decorate in honor of Saturn. (Blessedquietness.com)

Now that we have proven that the traditions are pagan and unacceptable for Covenant People to practice them and that Christmas is not the time of the birth of the Jewish Messiah, what shall we do with Christmas and especially with the Christmas Tree?

There were two trees in the Garden of Eden. One was the Tree of Life, and one was the Tree of Knowledge of Good and Evil. I call the Tree of Knowledge, the "Tree of Religion." Yeshua said, "I am the Way, the Truth and the Life." King David said, "Your Torah is a Tree of Life." Yeshua is the Living Torah as He is The Word made flesh. The Torah, *Pentateuch* or the Five Books, is the blueprint and foundation of the entire Bible! Yeshua is the Torah made flesh. He is the Tree of Life. In that context would you say that Christmas is from the Tree of Life or the Tree of Knowledge, the Tree of Death? What is the most prominent symbol of Christmas?

The Christmas Tree.

Interestingly, the many Founding Fathers of America and till 1870, forbade the celebration of Christmas, calling it a pagan feast. People were mandated to work on the 25th of December. Those who celebrated Christmas were penalized. It is not a secret that Christmas is pagan, that it is not Messiah's date birth, that the traditions are pagan, so why are those who consider themselves believers and disciples of Messiah still celebrating it? And why are they still putting Christmas trees in their homes and churches? Why do they continue marketing and propagating a *lie*? Why can't we forsake these pagan ways?

> **Destroy completely all the places on the high mountains and on the hills and under every spreading tree where the nations you are dispossessing worship their gods. Break down their altars, smash their sacred stones and burn their Asherah poles in the fire; cut down the idols of their gods and wipe out their names from those places. You must not worship the LORD your God in their way**
>
> — Deuteronomy 12:2-4

> **Thus says the LORD: "Do not learn the way of the Gentiles; Do not be dismayed at the signs of heaven for the Gentiles are dismayed at them. For the customs of the peoples fare futile; for one cuts a tree from the forest, The work of the hands of the workman, with the ax. They decorate it with silver and gold; they fasten it with nails and hammers So that it will not topple."**
>
> — Jeremiah 10:2-4

RELIGION OR HOLINESS?

> Pursue peace with all people, and holiness, without which no one will see the Lord.
> — Hebrews 12:14

Have we been called to uphold religious traditions borrowed from the pagans and Babylonians, or are we to affect this worldly society with *Holy Worship?* And what is Holiness? In Hebrew *kedusha* means "be separate," and to " touch no unclean thing."

> Thus you shall separate the children of Israel from their uncleanness, lest they die in their uncleanness when they defile My tabernacle that is among them.
> — Leviticus 15:31

This is confirmed in the New Testament:

> Therefore "Come out from among them and be separate, says the Lord. Do not touch what is unclean, and I will receive you."
> — 2 Corinthians 6:17

Are Roman Christmas traditions pagan and unclean? They were designed to worship Jupiter, Zeus, the sun god, and not the *Son of God*! Are we going to impact this society by "blending in" or by being *different* in their midst? The Cultural Gospel has been polluting the Church from the 4th Century until today, and the Holy One is calling us to repent and return to the *truth*. It is time to forsake the pagan traditions and feasts and come to celebrate the Holy Feasts as written in Leviticus 23.

> And the LORD spoke to Moses, saying, "Speak to the children of Israel, and say to them: 'The feasts of the LORD, which you shall proclaim to be holy convocations, these are My feasts.'"
> — Leviticus 23:1-2

Then Yah enumerates them: Shabbat, Passover, First Fruits, Feast of Weeks, Feast of Trumpets, Day of Atonement, and Feast of Tabernacles.

Each one of them testifies of who the Messiah is. He was not born at the time of a pagan celebration to Zeus. He was born, died and was resurrected at a Holy Season prescribed by the Father and He is calling us back to Holy Worship:

> But the time is coming—indeed it's here now—when true worshipers will worship the Father in spirit and in truth. The Father is looking for those who will worship him that way.
> — John 4:23

CHAPTER 10

CHRISTMAS IN SUKKOT?
AN URGENT PROPHETIC WARNING

> Now this I pray, that your love might overflow still more and more in knowledge and depth of discernment, in order to approve what is excellent—so that in the Day of Messiah you may be sincere and blameless.
>
> — *Philippians 1:9-10*

---

*C*AN IT BE that the birth of the Jewish Messiah did not happen on the 25th of December, the pagan Sun Worship feast of *Saturnalia*, but rather during the Biblical Feast of *Sukkot* (Tabernacles) in the Fall?

> **Then all the survivors from all the nations that attacked Jerusalem will go up from year to year to worship the King, A**DONAI**-Tzva'ot, and**

to celebrate Sukkot. Furthermore, if any of the nations on earth do not go up to Jerusalem to worship the King, Adonai-Tzva'ot, they will have no rain.

— Zechariah 14:16-17

Should we start a *revolution* all over the nations that celebrate a pagan feast with pagan traditions like the decorating of trees, carousing, and drinking? Should we *proclaim, publish*, and *broadcast*, to be heard *loud and clear*, that there is absolutely no fellowship between light and darkness and that the Holy Jewish Messiah does not partake of the table of demons?

Hear the word that Adonai speaks to you, house of Israel, Thus says Adonai: "Do not learn the way of the nations or be frightened by signs of the heavens—though the nations are terrified by them The customs of the peoples are useless: it is just a tree cut from the forest, the work of the hands of a craftsman with a chisel They decorate it with silver and gold, and fasten it with hammer and nails so it won't totter.

— Jeremiah 10:1-4

Should we cause such a stir? Why? Isn't it more comfortable to "go with the flow" and continue accommodating a 1,800-year lie established by the Roman-Byzantine Emperor Constantine, a Sun worshiper to the day of his death who was proclaimed to be the first Pope? Should we continue accommodating the pagan feasts that he instituted and the Christianity that he brought forth, completely divorced and disconnected from its original Jewish roots and Hebrew foundations? Should we just "let things be" for the sake of 'peace' whether the Holy God of Israel likes it or not? Should we continue perpetuating a *lie* that has allured the masses into a pagan celebration by the name of Christmas, that has absolutely *nothing* to do with the birth of the Jewish Messiah?

For what partnership is there between righteousness and lawlessness? Or what fellowship does light have with darkness?
— 2 Corinthians 6:14

Why would we stir up so much trouble by insisting that the Church worldwide *must* repent of their pagan holidays and traditions? What is the *big deal* with a little bit of paganism or a *lot* of it? Besides, we can surely redeem these pagan dates and dress them as "holy," can't we?

Woe to those who call evil good, and good evil; Who substitute darkness for light and light for darkness; Who substitute bitter for sweet, and sweet for bitter!
— Isaiah 5:20

AFTER ASKING SO MANY QUESTIONS, LET ME GIVE YOU THE PLAIN, SIMPLE, BIBLICAL ANSWER ON THIS

The very word "*answer*" is the Hebrew word *teshuva* which means both "answer" *and* "repentance." So, the answer is repentance!

The Hebrew word *teshuva* also means "returning to be restored."

If we want Christians, believers in the Jewish Messiah worldwide, to be *restored* then we all must *return* to the *original* Gospel made in Zion – pre-Constantine! The original Gospel comes from Jewish roots and contains Holy Worship and Biblical Feasts that YHVH calls His *"Moadim"* (His Feasts that *testify* of His greatness: Read Leviticus 23). We must return to the Jewish Messiah, the Lion from the Tribe of Judah and to Jerusalem, who is the Mother of the Nations, leaving Rome behind:

> Repent, therefore, and return—so your sins might be blotted out, so times of relief might come from the presence of Adonai and He might send Yeshua, the Messiah appointed for you. heaven must receive Him, until the time of the restoration of all the things that God spoke about long ago through the mouth of His holy prophets.
> — Acts 3:19-21

THE JEWISH ANSWER IS ALWAYS A QUESTION

> Yeshua replied to them, "I also will ask you one question. If you tell Me, I likewise will tell you by what authority I do these things.
> — Matthew 21:24

Why should we *not* return to the *original* Gospel and Biblical Worship and Feasts? Can you find *why not?*

Is it uncomfortable? Is it inconvenient? Can it ruffle feathers? Oh yes, but is it the *right* thing to do? Is it what YHVH prescribed in His Word? Will it bring salvation, miracles, and restoration worldwide? *Oh yes*!

> But an hour is coming—it is here now—when the true worshipers will worship the Father in spirit and truth, for the Father is seeking such people as His worshipers.
> — John 4:23

WORSHIPPERS IN SPIRIT AND TRUTH ARE CALLED TO THE END-TIME ARMY OF GOD!

So now all that is left is a *choice: Your choice*, your family's choice, your church's choice, your denomination's choice.

If you belong to Yeshua, the Jewish Messiah (although you may have called Him by the Greek name of Jesus, which is *not* His God-given name!), then *do what is right*. He is not pleased with those that do not. And while you are at it, why continue calling Him by the Greco-pagan name? Why not call Him *Yeshua*, the name given to Him by His Father, the God of Israel? After all, it is to His original name (pre-Constantine) that *every* knee shall bow!

> "Do not think that I came to abolish the Torah or the Prophets! I did not come to abolish, but to fulfill. Amen, I tell you, until heaven and earth pass away, not the smallest letter or serif shall ever pass away from the Torah until all things come to pass. Therefore, whoever breaks one of the least of these commandments, and teaches others the same, shall be called least in the kingdom of heaven. But whoever keeps and teaches them, this one shall be called great in the kingdom of heaven. For I tell you that unless your righteousness exceeds that of the Pharisees and Torah scholars, you shall never enter the kingdom of heaven!
>
> — Matthew 5:17-20

If you belong to the Greek god Jesus Christ, who has been preached by Constantine, with pagan feasts and hatred against the Jews and everything Jewish, including Torah and Biblical Feasts, you can continue to stay with all your pagan celebrations, but with these the devil is well pleased, and of course, everyone will love you. But beware of what Yeshua says about it through the Jewish Apostle Paul:

> You cannot drink the cup of the LORD and the cup of demons. You cannot partake of the table of the LORD and the table of demons.
>
> — 1 Corinthians 10:21

If you consider yourself to be a Bishop, Pastor, or any Spiritual Leader, please remember that you will give an *account* to the Judge of *All* about *what* you have been teaching and *why*. If you are afraid to lose 'your' sheep you'd better *wake* up! Remember the people who are under your care are *not yours*. YHVH is calling *all* to repent and to be *restored* to the *original* Gospel of the Kingdom with Jewish roots and Hebrew foundations:

> "When he has brought out all his own, he goes ahead of them; and the sheep follow him because they know his voice. They will never follow a stranger, but will run away from him, for they do not know the voice of strangers."
>
> — John 10:4-6

And *if* you are so *lukewarm* that you are trying to please the devil and the people by continuing pagan feasts and celebrations, with pagan traditions that you know very well *are* pagan, then remember that He said He will *vomit* you out of His *mouth* and that the fear of man is a *snare*:

> Fear of man will prove to be a snare, but one who trusts in ADONAI will be kept safe.
>
> — Proverbs 29:25

THIS MESSAGE IS A SERIOUS PROPHETIC WARNING!

Judgment has begun in the House of ADONAI, and this is a matter of *life and death:*

> For the time has come for judgment to begin with the house of God. If judgment begins with us first, what will be the end for those who disobey the Good News of God?
>
> — 1 Peter 4:17

Whom should we please? The religious traditions? The comfort zones of people? The nice family memories? The lukewarm preachers? *Or should we please YHVH and Him alone?*

And whom should we *fear?* Should we fear those who will persecute us for doing what is right (*feasts, morality, justice*) in Yah's eyes, those that can even kill us for preaching the true Gospel of the Kingdom as the Original Jewish Apostles taught? Or should we fear the *only* one that can both kill the body and throw our soul into hell?

> And do not fear those who kill the body but cannot kill the soul. Instead, fear the One who is able to destroy both soul and body in Gehenna.
>
> — Matthew 10:28

TOO STRONG A MESSAGE FOR YOU?

Have you *read* the Bible lately? And have you *communed* with the Holy Spirit who is the Spirit of Holiness recently? *What is he saying?*

* Read my book *The Healing Power of the Roots* to see more about how: www.kad-esh.org/shop

Therefore, everyone who hears these words of Mine and acts on them, may be compared to a wise man who built his house on the rock. And the rain fell, and the floods came, and the winds blew and slammed against that house; and yet it did not fall, for it had been founded on the rock. Everyone who hears these words of Mine and does not act on them, will be like a foolish man who built his house on the sand. The rain fell, and the floods came, and the winds blew and slammed against that house; and it fell—and great was its fall."

— Matthew 7:24-27

It is time to *repent*, do *teshuva*, *return*, and *be restored*! A Great Awakening is knocking at the door; the salvation of all nations is at stake:

Then I saw another angel flying in midair, and he had the eternal gospel to proclaim to those who live on the earth—to every nation, tribe, language and people. He said in a loud voice, "Fear God and give him glory, because the hour of his judgment has come. Worship him who made the heavens, the earth, the sea and the springs of water." A second angel followed and said, "'Fallen! Fallen is Babylon the Great,' which made all the nations drink the maddening wine of her adulteries."

— Revelation 14:6-8

And this gospel of the kingdom will be preached in the whole world as a testimony to all nations, and then the end will come.

— Matthew 24:14

CHAPTER 11

HANUKKAH TIME
A CALL FOR REDEDICATION AND EXPANSION

> Rise up! Consecrate the people and say, 'Consecrate yourselves for tomorrow, for thus YHVH, the God of Israel, has said, "There are things under the ban in your midst, O Israel. You cannot stand before your enemies until you have removed the things under the ban from your midst.
>
> — *Joshua 7:13*

---

*W*E HAVE ALREADY entered the year of 5779 in the Hebrew Calendar and are about to enter the year of 2019 in the Gregorian Calendar. We are living in such Prophetic timings! The U.N. *is trying to divide and destroy Israel as I write, but YHVH will fight for us as He promised and as you pray:*

> In that day YHVH will defend the inhabitants of Jerusalem, and the one who is feeble among them in that day will be like David, and the house of David will be like God, like the angel of YHVH before them. And in that day I will set about to destroy all the nations that come against Jerusalem.
>
> — Zechariah 12:8-9

We know that we have but a short time while it is still day to work, then the night comes when no one can work.

GLOBAL AWAKENING TIME

Our Jewish Messiah needs to rule in *all* countries, and it is time; indeed, it is high time for a *worldwide awakening* in the Church! *Teshuva* – returning to the original Gospel made in Zion, with Jewish roots and the love of Israel as the *key* for this awakening. *Many people are crying out for revival, but this revival will be different. YHVH is calling us to get rid of all Babylonian feasts and remove everything that offends Him in our system of worship.*

> Then Adonai said to Joshua, "Arise! Why are you fallen on your face? Israel has sinned. Yes, they have also transgressed My covenant, which I commanded them. Now they have even taken of the things under the ban of destruction
>
> — Joshua 7:10-11

Just like Israel with *Ai* (see Joshua 7-8), we cannot stand and prevail against the enemy when there is sin in the camp. *Achan* had hidden a Babylonian garment under his tent. *In the same way Replacement Theology with Pagan Feasts and*

Babylonian traditions, like Christmas trees, are buried inside the Church in America and all nations.

SEE 'GIFTS UNDER TREES' AS A PAGAN TRADITION

> When I had brought them into the land which I swore to give to them, then they saw every high hill and every leafy tree, and they offered there their sacrifices and there they presented the provocation of their offering. There also they made their soothing aroma and there they poured out their drink offerings.
>
> — Ezekiel 20:28

SEE 'DECORATING TREES' AS AN ACT OF WORSHIP THAT IS A PAGAN TRADITION

> "Do not learn the way of the nations, and do not be terrified by the signs of the heavens although the nations are terrified by them; For the customs of the peoples are delusion; because it is wood cut from the forest, the work of the hands of a craftsman with a cutting tool. "They decorate it with silver and with gold; they fasten it with nails and with hammers so that it will not totter.
>
> — Jeremiah 10:1-4

THE ACHAN SYNDROME IN THE CHURCH (JOSHUA 7)

Israel could not stand or prevail against her enemies as long as there were pagan things buried in their tents. Pagan feasts and traditions have been coveted and buried in the Church for too long! Did you know than in America, it was forbidden to celebrate Christmas, as it was a pagan feast with pagan traditions, imported from the Greco-Babylonian-Roman-European-Scandinavian pagan worship system?

WHEN WAS CHRISTMAS ILLEGAL IN THE UNITED STATES?

In Colonial America, the Puritans of New England disapproved of Christmas, and its celebration was outlawed in Boston from 1659 to 1681. The ban by the Pilgrims was revoked by English governor Edmund Andros, however, it was not until the mid-19th Century that celebrating Christmas became fashionable in the Boston region. (Barnett, Marling, TIME.com)

A MATTER OF LIFE AND DEATH

In 1994 Yeshua spoke to me that preaching the Jewish roots to the Church is a *matter of life and death*. (See my book *The Healing Power of the Roots*.) Ever since, I have been *agonizing* over finding a way to make this urgent message known to *every* person on the planet.

We have opened a way where there was no way, against all the odds, with Israeli like *Hutspah* (nerve, boldness), and persistence. It was *against all the odds* that we started to broadcast on T.V. Every day we would watch the bank account and see that there was not enough money to pay for those programs, and yet at the last moment, an offering would come and help us hit the target. HalelluYAH!

YOUR SEEDS ARE LIKE THE DEW OF THE MORNING TO OUR SOULS. THANK YOU!

Now we must expand! We must make sure that *every person* hears the true "Gospel made in Zion," with Jewish roots, Holiness and Righteousness, Holy Feasts, the name of Yeshua, the love of Israel, with *signs, wonders* and *miracles* following!

> "The Church is like a Rose cut off from her garden and put in a vase of water for 2 days, and on the 3rd Day, if she is not replanted back, she will surely die."*

We are on the 3rd Day, the 3rd Millennium and the Church must be *replanted back, grafted in,* into the Jewish roots and Foundations, into the name of Yeshua and the Gospel Made in Zion:

> But if some of the branches were broken off and you—being a wild olive—were grafted in among them and became a partaker of the root of the olive tree with its richness, do not boast against the branches. But if you do boast, it is not you who support the root but the root supports you. You will say then, "Branches were broken off so that I might be grafted in." True enough. They were broken off because of unbelief, and you stand by faith. Do not be arrogant, but fear— for if God did not spare the natural branches, neither will He spare you.
>
> — Romans 11:17-21

We are now taking a step of *faith*, a leap of faith to *expand all our operations to touch every person possible and quickly*. We will be using Social Media like never before, press releases, T.V.

---

* Bierman, Dominiquae. *The Healing Power of the Roots*

programs, and T.V. interviews. It is *very costly* to do so, both personally and financially, but for us, it would be *much more expensive* if we fail to do so.

I could not face the Messiah giving Him excuses of why the urgent message He has given me has not been heard *loud and clear*.

Here is our commitment to *you* and Yah: *Expansion with no limitations*. The 3rd Day *Revival* is *around the corner*!

We invite you to expand with us. Expand your heart, your giving, and your prayers. The Holy Spirit coupled with your faithfulness and love is the wind beneath our wings and is the fuel of this ministry.

AS YOU PARTNER WITH US:

May YHVH bless your seed to multiply into the thousands and tens of thousands, and may you possess the gates of all your enemies in Yeshua's Mighty Name!

> **They blessed Rebekah and said to her, "May you, our sister, become thousands of ten thousands, and may your descendants possess the gate of those who hate them."**
> **— Genesis 24:60**

CHAPTER 12

THE HANUKKAH TURNING POINT
A PROPHETIC MESSAGE FOR THE SEASON

> But he answered and said unto them, why do ye also transgress the commandment of God by your tradition?
>
> — *Matthew 15:3 KJV*

---

*T*HIS HANUKKAH IS a turning point in time for the Church. YHVH is calling us to rededicate our lives and style of worship to Him! The battle was very fierce for the Jewish Priests, the Maccabees that defied the fearsome Greco-Syrian Empire. They knew that they needed to fight this battle to the death and take the Holy Temple back from paganism. In the same way, the campaign to rededicate the Body of Messiah to Holy Worship from Roman-Babylonian influences is fierce. The enemy thinks he has the upper hand since the Church has been divorced from its Jewish roots since the Council of Nicaea in 325 A.D.

How can things suddenly change if, for 1,700 years or so, the Church has been celebrating pagan feasts instead of Holy worship?

But you will be amazed at how YHVH can bring about a great victory once He finds a group of *committed* Royal Priests to be willing to lay down their lives! He will back them up all the way, and He will make a way where there seems to be no way:

> Then he said to me, "This is the word of the LORD to Zerubbabel saying, 'Not by might nor by power, but by My Spirit," says the LORD of hosts. "What are you, O great mountain? Before Zerubbabel you will become a plain; and he will bring forth the top stone with shouts of "Grace, grace to it!"'
>
> — Zechariah 4:6

FROM ROME TO JERUSALEM

Yeshua wants His Bride to return to Jerusalem from Rome. He wants His Bride purified from sun worship and pagan traditions prevalent in Christmas and Easter. It is *He* who is reclaiming His Temple! But He needs us, a Royal Priesthood like *Zadok**, to teach the people to distinguish between the holy and the profane. He needs some Holy Priests that are not afraid of men! You see, many preachers know that it is time to forsake Rome and go back to the Hebrew foundations of the Gospel. Many pastors know that Yeshua is the true and eternal name of the Messiah. Many leaders know that Christmas trees

---

* Righteous priesthood, see 1 Samuel 2:35; Ezekiel 44:23.

and Easter bunny eggs are from pagan worship. Many already know that Yeshua was not born on Christmas or resurrected on Easter (the celebration of the goddess of fertility *Ishtar*). So why on earth are they continuing to feed their flock with that which is abominable to YHVH? This *deception* is a very grievous sin beloved ones, and YHVH is about to judge His Body on this:

> **For it is time for judgment to begin with the household of God; and if it begins with us first, what will be the outcome for those who do not obey the gospel of God? And if it is with difficulty that the righteous is saved, what will become of the godless man and the sinner?**
> **— 1 Peter 4:17-18**

If we know something is wrong, why do we continue to do it? The definition of *insanity is* "to keep on doing the same thing and expect a different result." Continuing to walk in sin and expect a true *revival* is insanity! Do leaders continue walking in the ways of Rome out of the fear of men, the fear of losing members, the fear of losing tithes or all of the above? And if so, can the Almighty excuse us? Can He excuse those pastors and leaders that keep feeding their flock with pagan garbage? Is it not *high time* to *wake up* and *repent* beloved? Or do we need to continue being "diplomatic" about it when the whole world is steeped in sin and immorality, and the Church is no better?

TURNING POINT THIS HANUKKAH

At that time the Feast of the Dedication (Hanukkah) took place at Jerusalem; it was winter, and Yeshua was walking in the temple in the portico of Solomon.

— John 10:22-23

This Hanukkah, the Feast of Dedication, when Yeshua revealed Himself as the Messiah in Jerusalem is a Feast of Turning Point. Currently (at the time of this writing), it is the Biblical Year of 5779, and it is a particular year of grace for the *repentant*.

Mark my words: A great shaking is coming, a falling away. It has been going on for quite a while in many churches, but it will increase. There is an onslaught of the enemy, and the Church cannot stand as it is weakened by pagan traditions and immorality. It cannot stand when the preachers are broadcasting a cheap grace gospel that carries no consequences, and true prophets are banned or silenced.

At the time of Joshua, the people of Israel could not stand in battle against their enemies because they had a Babylonian garment that was banned, hidden under the tent of Achan from the Tribe of Judah. When we have pagan stuff in our lives, hidden things in the closet, pagan traditions we refuse to let go of, idolatry, immorality, hatred, unforgiveness, pride and stubbornness of heart can we stand before our enemies?

We have grieved the Precious Holy Spirit tremendously by rejecting all the revelation that we have received about Replacement Theology and the need to *forsake* it *entirely*.

Fully forsaking Replacement Theology includes abandoning pagan festivals like Christmas, Easter, and Sun (worship) Day. We can do evangelistic outreach on those days, but we must not celebrate them with pagan traditions or propagate the lie that Yeshua was born on Christmas. We must refuse to spread the myth that it is *ok* to dress pagan feast in "Christian garb." Is it ok to dress a pig as a lamb or a scorpion as a butterfly? The wolf in *The Little Red Riding Hood* was disguised as grandma, but he was still a wolf and attacked the girl anyway! There is a profound reason that until 1870 the puritans in Boston forbade the celebration of Christmas and people were heavily fined if found violating that ban. They knew it was pagan:

> Rise up! Consecrate the people and say, 'Consecrate yourselves for tomorrow, for thus the Lord, the God of Israel, has said, "There are things under the ban in your midst, O Israel. You cannot stand before your enemies until you have removed the things under the ban from your midst.
>
> — Joshua 7:13

WHY NOT SIMPLY OBEY GOD?

But now, in our "modern times," we have become like those living in the ancient times of Constantine and the Roman Empire: Everything goes, and if it "feels good" do it. People defend themselves by saying, "I do not worship the Christmas Tree." Although they know it is a pagan tradition, they continue celebrating it because of nostalgic sentiments or to blend in. *If you do not worship the tree, why do you still decorate it and fasten it on the altar of your home, T.V. studio, business, and Church if YHVH said not to do it?* If you do not worship it, then just let it go because God said so! Or is it being too religious for us to obey the God of the Bible?

> Do not learn the way of the nations, and do not be terrified by the signs of the heavens although the nations are terrified by them; For the customs of the peoples are delusion; because it is wood cut from the forest, the work of the hands of a craftsman with a cutting tool. "They decorate it with silver and with gold; they fasten it with nails and with hammers so that it will not totter.
>
> — Jeremiah 10:1-4

CIRCUMCISION OF THE HEART

These Eight Days of Hanukkah are days of *Circumcision of the Heart*! As you light up your Hanukkah Menorah check and see that there are no hidden or overt things that are grieving the Holy Spirit. Repent, renounce them, command all unclean spirits out of your life, and go ahead, *rededicate* your life to the Jewish Messiah in holiness and righteousness.

I hope that next year there will not be a Christmas tree in your home or church, as we all celebrate Hanukkah together with Yeshua who celebrated the Feast of Dedication in Jerusalem and said the following words:

> My sheep hear My voice, and I know them, and they follow Me.
>
> — John 10:27

PART B
TRUTH AND LIES

CHAPTER 13

BLOWING THE DUST OFF THE TRUTH
EXPOSING FATAL LIES

> And you will know the truth,
> and the truth will make you free.
>
> — *John 8:32*

---

*A*LL OF MANKIND FELL because *Adam* believed one lie, so believing lies can cause us to fall from grace.

The serpent said to the woman, "You surely will not die!"
— **Genesis 3:4**

Sin only followed the belief in a lie. When the woman heard the snake, she believed the lie that their disobedience to ELOHIM's Commandments would carry no consequences. She also thought that the Tree of Knowledge was "good" though the Creator had said it was deathly. When we believe in a lie it can cost us our life as it leads us to sin and the wages of sin (breaking ELOHIM's Commandments) is *death*:

> **For the wages of sin is death, but the free gift of God is eternal life in Messiah Yeshua our Lord.**
>
> **— Romans 6:23**

In the course of my 25 years of serving Yeshua, I have come across many lies that have become deathly doctrines. The most dangerous myths are those that happen because of mistranslation of the Bible or due to biased translation. I will bring a few serious examples here.

THE POSITION OF MAN

> **What is man that You take thought of him, and the son of man (Adam) that You care for him? Yet You have made him a little lower than God (Elohim),**
>
> **— Psalm 8:4-5**

The position of Adam (man and woman) is a "little lower" than ELOHIM as they are created in the image and likeness of ELOHIM:

> **Elohim created man in His own image, in the image of Elohim-God He created him; male and female He created them.**
>
> **— Genesis 1:27**

In many translations it says:

For thou hast made him a little lower than the angels, and hast crowned him with glory and honour.

— Psalm 8:5 KJV

In Hebrew, *Elohim* is the term for the Creator and *Malachim* is the word for angels, why would the translator of such a well-read Bible translate Elohim as angels? Because of the doctrines of demons and men that entered the Church through Replacement Theology! If humanity that is created in the image and likeness of Elohim is a little lower than the angels, that means that Lucifer (Satan) who is a fallen angel – is greater than Adam, and thus greater than Elohim Himself.

> "How you have fallen from heaven, O star of the morning, son of the dawn! You have been cut down to the earth, You who have weakened the nations! But you said in your heart, 'I will ascend to heaven; I will raise my throne above the stars of God, and I will sit on the mount of assembly in the recesses of the north. I will ascend above the heights of the clouds; I will make myself like the Most High.'"
>
> — Isaiah 14:12-14

Yeshua said:

> And he said unto them, I beheld Satan as lightning fall from heaven. Behold, I give unto you power to tread on serpents and scorpions, and over all the power of the enemy: and nothing shall by any means hurt you.
>
> — Luke 10:18-19

You and I are created *higher* than all the angels! That is why we can have authority over demons that are fallen angels. The only reason that Adam (male and female) lost their authority was because they believed a lie and sinned. If we believe the truth and obey ELOHIM, we too have authority over the angels.

> Do you not know that we will judge angels? How much more matters of this life?
> — 1 Corinthians 6:3

DISCRIMINATION AGAINST WOMEN

> The LORD gives the command; the women who proclaim the good tidings are a great host:
> — Psalm 68:11

In Hebrew, it says that the women who preach, proclaim and declare the Good News are a great army. The name for "women preachers or evangelists" used in Hebrew is *mevasrot*. There is no option to translate it any other way. However in the King James Version which has been the most prevalent version of the Bible in English it says *those* instead of "the women." This change is on purpose: To remove any traces of female gender in the very clear calling for women to be preachers and evangelists and preach the Gospel!

> The LORD gave the word: great was the company of those that published it.
> — Psalm 68:11 KJV

This fatal error is due to the bias of the translators against Women, which has caused untold wrongs in the Church since the Council of Nicaea and on. Tremendous abuses against women and even murder in religious circles have happened due to these doctrines of demons and men! Many women worldwide are prevented from obeying the high call of Yah (God) because of these fatal lies.

Another purposeful mistranslation concerning women occurs in the New Testament:

> **Greet Andronicus and Junias, my kinsmen and my fellow prisoners, who are outstanding among the apostles, who also were in Christ before me.**
>
> — Romans 16:7

Even a relatively accurate translation like the New American Standard is not perfect and here we find a change of name. The original Greek says, "Greet Andronicus and Junia." Junia is the name of a woman in Greek and Junias is the name of a man. *The name of this outstanding woman apostle was changed because it did not fit the theology of the translators.*

Interestingly enough, the King James Version does leave the original name of the woman Apostle Junia in it:

> **Salute Andronicus and Junia, my kinsmen, and my fellow-prisoners, who are of note among the apostles, who also were in Christ before me.**
>
> — Romans 16:7 KJV

Check your bibles in different versions and languages and see what they say, you will find many surprises that are fatal lies that lead to deathly doctrines. This particular woman Apostle was actually a believer before Paul got saved and had suffered a lot for the Gospel.

We salute Junia!

"WOMEN SHOULD NOT TEACH MEN"

Another demonic doctrine made out of biased translation:

> But I suffer not a woman to teach, nor to usurp authority over the man, but to be in silence.
>
> — 1 Timothy 2:12 KJV

> But I suffer not a woman to teach, nor to usurp authority over the man, but to be in silence.
>
> — 1 Timothy 2:12

Here both translations have translated a Greek word in a biased way. The word for "usurp authority" here in Greek is *autenteo*. This word is not used anywhere else in the New Testament, and it does not mean "usurp authority" but rather, "influence a man through sexual manipulation."

At that time that Apostle Paul wrote a pastoral letter to Pastor Timothy, many of the prostitutes at the Temple of Diana were being saved. They were very "savvy" and very charismatic. They were used to manipulating men with their sexuality. So, Paul was warning Timothy that these women needed to get cleansed and delivered before they could teach others.

This verse should have been translated as follows: "*But I suffer not a convert from the temple prostitutes to teach and disturb a service, nor to influence men through sexual manipulation, but to be in silence until they are set free and walk in holiness.*"

That is a far cry from silencing all women and preventing women from teaching doctrine or entering leadership positions!

Deborah, the Prophetess, taught the Sons of Israel Torah. She was the ruler and king of the hour. Surely the women in the New Covenant should be free to do like-wise when called.

> Now Deborah, a prophetess, the wife of Lappidoth, was judging Israel at that time. She used to sit under the palm tree of Deborah between Ramah and Bethel in the hill country of Ephraim; and the sons of Israel came up to her for judgment.
> — Judges 4:4-5

REPLACING THE JEWS

> But if some of the branches were broken off, and you, being a wild olive, were grafted in among them and became partaker with them of the rich root of the olive tree, do not be arrogant toward the branches; but if you are arrogant, remember that it is not you who supports the root, but the root supports you.
> — Romans 11:17-18

Above it reads that the Gentiles (wild branches) are grafted in *among* the natural (Jewish) branches and they become partakers *with* them of the rich root of the Olive Tree (Covenant Promises). Of course, this is totally right, Gentiles have *no* covenant with ELOHIM, only Israel and Judah do, so without the "natural branches" there is no covenant for the Gentiles. There is no "Old Covenant" for the Gentiles and no "New Covenant" either! In other words the wild branches (Gentiles) join the Jewish Olive Tree and not vice versa.

But in some languages like in Spanish *Reina Valera* Bible (King James) that is used by most Christians, it does not say "grafted in among them" but rather "Grafted in *instead* of them." (check your bibles and translations)

Que si algunas de las ramas fueron quebradas, y tú, siendo acebuche, has sido injertado en lugar de ellas, y has sido hecho participante de la raíz y de la grosura de la oliva;

What is very serious here is that even in later versions of Reina Valera 1995, it is still the same and it says *instead* of them. This means that the deathly Replacement Theology is "alive and well" in the Christian Church of today!

Many years ago, I was preaching in Lima, Peru, and exposing this lie in their most revered Bible, which is *Reina Valera*. As I was explaining how a lie like this can affect all your doctrine to become anti-Jewish, the pastor got so offended with me for telling him that "his bible" was wrong, that he ordered us out of there and forbade the sales of any of my books! The people that had their eyes opened tried to get my books in the midst of the rush of us being pushed out of there and the Pastor's wife that had much more sense than her husband, managed to purchase a large quantity of my book *Grafted In* so she could teach the truth in the Bible School that she was in charge of.

It is very important that we do not worship any translation but rather get our undiluted doctrine from the original Scriptures in Hebrew and Greek, taking into consideration the historical background, the integrity of Scripture and the revelation of the Holy Spirit.

> All Scripture is inspired by God and profitable for teaching, for reproof, for correction, for training in righteousness.
>
> — 2 Timothy 3:16

It's interesting to note that when the above word was written from Paul to Timothy, the only Scripture available was what many call the "Old Testament." The New Testament was canonized about 300 years later in 325 A.D. after the Council of Nicaea established Replacement Theology as Church doctrine. Something to think about! The original Apostles had their doctrine from the Hebrew Holy Scriptures, and they changed the world.

THE INTEGRITY OF SCRIPTURE

> This is the third time I am coming to you. every fact is to be confirmed by the testimony of two or three witnesses.
>
> — 2 Corinthians 13:1

It is clear to any true Bible Scholar that it is wrong to establish any doctrine based on one Scripture. However this principle has been grossly violated when it comes to baptism. Most of the Christians in the world are baptized in the name of the Father, Son, and Holy Spirit. That, of course, is a total deception as it is based on only *one* scripture! There is no other Scripture to confirm it, and there is no basis for establishing this as Church Doctrine, and *yet* millions have believed it is right.

> Go therefore and make disciples of all the nations, baptizing them in the name of the Father and the Son and the Holy Spirit.
>
> — Matthew 28:19

There are many scholars that believe that the Book of Matthew was originally in Hebrew and that the original manuscript is in the Vatican. Also that this particular Scripture was changed to support the doctrine of the Trinity that speaks about *three gods*. There is a *big* difference between Trinity (three separate gods) and Tri-unity. Tri-unity is one God that manifests Himself in three different but harmonious ways as the Father, the Son, and the Holy Spirit. ELOHIM in Hebrew is *plural,* but it is Echad, *One.*

Matthew 28:19 is the only Scripture in the New Testament that calls to be baptized in the name of the Father (YHVH), the Son (Yeshua), and the Holy Spirit (does not have a name but rather a function). *All* the other Scriptures throughout the Book of Acts call for baptism by full immersion into the name of Yeshua – into His death, burial, and resurrection. *The Father did not die, nor was buried or resurrected. Neither the Holy Spirit died, neither was buried and resurrected!*

The only one that died was the Son, Yeshua, the Messiah and we identify with Him, and we become *one* with Him through baptism to worship the Father in Spirit and Truth as we obey and are led by the Holy Spirit (John 4; Romans 8).

> **Therefore we have been buried with Him through baptism into death, so that as Christ was raised from the dead through the glory of the Father, so we too might walk in newness of life. For if we have become united with Him in the likeness of His death, certainly we shall also be in the likeness of His resurrection.**
>
> **— Romans 6:4-5**

Countless of Christians have been wrongly baptized because of a fatal lie based on the purposeful mistranslation of *one* Scripture because of the doctrines of demons and men:

> Peter said to them, "Repent, and each of you be baptized in the name of Yeshua the Messiah for the forgiveness of your sins; and you will receive the gift of the Holy Spirit."
> — Acts 2:38

> And he ordered them to be baptized in the name of Yeshua HaMashiach.
> — Acts 10:48

> When they heard this, they were baptized in the name of the Lord Yeshua.
> — Acts 19:5

FEAR NOT TO OBEY THE TRUTH!

Many people are afraid of the "Jesus only" cult, and that is why they refrain from being baptized into the name of Yeshua. *But is it right to continue in a lie for fear of another lie?* Two wrongs do not make a right. We must obey the truth though it may cost. The Spirit of Religion always fights against the Spirit of Truth.

> Buy truth, and do not sell it, get wisdom and instruction and understanding.
> — Proverbs 23:23

The verses are as they appear in any version of the New Covenant, with the only difference that I have taken the liberty to restore the true name of Messiah to the original one that *Abba* gave him through the Angel Gabriel when he spoke to Joseph.

THE CHANGE OF YESHUA'S NAME

Why would anyone change the name of the Messiah? The answer is simple: To hide His Jewish identity and create a universal Christ for all people. But He came in the flesh as a Jew and any other identity is from the Spirit of Anti-messiah:

> Beloved, do not believe every spirit, but test the spirits to see whether they are from God, because many false prophets have gone out into the world. By this you know the Spirit of God: every spirit that confesses that Yeshua the Messiah has come in the flesh is from God; and every spirit that does not confess Yeshua (as a human Jew) is not from God; this is the spirit of the antichrist, of which you have heard that it is coming, and now it is already in the world.
>
> — 1 John 4:1-13

After all, the name of *Buddha* does not need translation, neither the name of *Satan,* so why the name of *Yeshua* needs translation or rather transliteration?

> She will bear a Son; and you shall call His name Yeshua, for He will save His people from their sin.
>
> — Matthew 1:21

Yeshua in Hebrew means "salvation," but Jesus does not! Millions have been murdered in the name of Jesus Christ, but *no one* has ever been murdered in the name of Yeshua. Jesus

Christ is used as a cuss word in many movies, but the name of Yeshua has never been used as a cuss word. Yah has kept the actual name of His Son pure, and He is calling us to restore it.

For this I invite you to order my book, *Yeshua is the Name,* at www.kad-esh.org – Press on "Shop."

So that at the name of Yeshua every knee will bow, of those who are in heaven and on earth and under the earth,

– Philippians 2:10

Satan is deathly afraid of His true Name.

"THE JEWS KILLED CHRIST"

For this reason the Father loves Me, because I lay down My life so that I may take it again. No one has taken it away from Me, but I lay it down on My own initiative. I have authority to lay it down, and I have authority to take it up again. This commandment I received from My Father.

– John 10:17-18

Millions of Jews have been murdered because of the belief in this one lie; however, Yeshua said that *no one* could take His life. He laid it down on His own initiative. Yeshua was *not* murdered by Jews; He laid down His life as a sacrifice to bring both Jews and Gentiles, salvation!

On top of it the Jews could not "kill Christ" as they had no authority to execute the death penalty at that time. All of Israel was under the Roman Empire, and only the Romans had authority to execute criminals. That is why Yeshua was handed to Pilate, and he was nailed to the execution tree (Cross) by Roman soldiers and not by the Jews!

The bottom line is this: Yeshua died for the sins of Jews and Gentiles; without His sacrifice, there is no salvation. But how many Jews have been murdered in the name of Jesus Christ because of belief in this one lie—"The Jews killed Christ." Millions murdered; millions hated... that is what I call a fatal lie.

A UNITY ISSUE

One LORD, one faith, one baptism.

— Ephesians 4:4

Since Replacement Theology was established as Church Doctrine divorcing the 4th Century Church from everything Jewish and from Yeshua Himself, it has caused the lives of millions of people. The fatal lies that appear in translations have caused disunity and division. Just on the issue of baptism – people have died to reestablish baptism by full immersion! And today many people are afraid to cause contention if they mention that the baptism in the name of the Father, Son, and Holy Spirit is wrong. We are all called to only one baptism or one kind of baptism, and it is *into* the name of Yeshua. There is only *one* LORD, and He is a Jew. His name is Hebrew, and it is into His name that we are all called to be immersed; it is with Him that we need to become *one*. All our power, anointing, and authority come from the fact that we are *one* with Yeshua through the Blood of Yeshua and Baptism, or rather "*mikveh!*'"

MERCY!

The Almighty has been very merciful because of the ignorance of most of the Church, but there is no need to stay in ignorance any longer! Ignorance is darkness, and it causes people to believe in fables and superstitions.

There are not two different "gods," one of the Old Testament that is a god of judgment and one of the New Testament that is a god of grace. It's only *one* God, *one* LORD:

> Hear, O Israel! YHVH is our ELOHIM, YHVH is one! You shall love the LORD your God with all your heart and with all your soul and with all your might.
>
> — Deuteronomy 6: 4-5

There are not all kinds of baptisms, there is only *one,* and it is into the name of Yeshua. Even if you are rededicating your life and your baptism, it is still *one* and into the name of Yeshua. You can go into the water seven times if you want, but it's into the name of Yeshua.

There is only *one* faith, and it was handed to the Jewish apostles 2,000 years ago. It is the Gospel "made in Zion," not in Babylon or Rome or even Germany with Martin Luther.

YHVH is calling all of us to be sanctified by the truth, so we may be *one,* and so the world can believe.

---

* Mikveh: A Jewish ritual immersion for purification and sanctification, normally in a pool or a body of living water; original Biblical baptism.

> Sanctify them in the truth; Your word is truth. As You sent Me into the world, I also have sent them into the world. For their sakes I sanctify Myself, that they themselves also may be sanctified in truth. "I do not ask on behalf of these alone, but for those also who believe in Me through their word; that they may all be one; even as You, Father, are in Me and I in You, that they also may be in Us, so that the world may believe that You sent Me.
>
> — John 17:17-21

Time is *very* late, and the sanctification of the Bride of Messiah from fatal lies is *urgent*.

Here I have touched some core issues that have caused misery to millions of people, and that has diminished the authority and the glory that we walk in. It is time to stop all theological debates and to *repent* so we can be sanctified by the truth and we can be *one*. A desperately wicked and dying world and all creation are waiting on us, Jew and Gentile to become *one* in Messiah and to manifest His glory. Fatal lies are separating and dividing Jews, Gentiles, men, and women. May we love *truth* above our traditions.

> So that He might sanctify her, having cleansed her by the washing of water with the word, that He might present to Himself the church in all her glory, having no spot or wrinkle or any such thing; but that she would be holy and blameless.
>
> — Ephesians 5:26-27

WHO IS YESHUA?

> And the Word became flesh and dwelt among us.
> — John 1:14

Many of the Messianic believers are falling into the deception that Yeshua is not YHVH-God! This same kind of deception was in effect in the 2nd Century B.C. through a false doctrine called *Marcionism*. It was because of this that the doctrine of the Trinity took root; to counteract Marcionism and the fact that many believers were opposing the divinity of Yeshua. I want to establish a point here, and it is straightforward: Denying His divinity or His humanity are *both* deceptions!

YESHUA IS THE WORD MADE INTO A JEW

For the most part, the Gentile Christians through Replacement Theology have denied His Humanity as being a *Jew* and created a Universal Christ instead of a Jewish Messiah. That deception is born of the very spirit of Anti-messiah or Antichrist as many call it:

> And every spirit that does not confess that Yeshua HaMashiach has come in the flesh (as a Jew) is not of God. And this is the spirit of the Antichrist, which you have heard was coming, and is now already in the world.
> — 1 John 4:3

Every spirit that does not acknowledge that Yeshua came in the flesh, as a man, as a Jewish man is of the spirit of Anti-messiah. That is why Replacement Theology validated by the Council of Nicaea sought to eradicate all traces of the

Jewishness of Yeshua by replacing His name for a Greek name, the Biblical-Hebrew Feasts for pagan feasts, the Shabbat for Sunday, and the Torah for twisted interpretations of the New Testament. Those changes were wholly divorced from the blueprint in the Hebrew Holy Scriptures that was deceptively called "Old Testament" but Paul called it the Holy Scriptures:

> **And that from childhood you have known the Holy Scriptures, which are able to make you wise for salvation through faith which is in Messiah Yeshua.**
>
> **— 2 Timothy 3:15**

Yeshua was born as a Jewish man, rose from the dead as a glorified Jewish man, and is in heaven as a Jewish Lion. A Jew will judge all humanity!

> **But one of the elders said to me, "Do not weep. Behold, the Lion of the tribe of Judah, the Root of David, has prevailed to open the scroll and to loose its seven seals."**
>
> **— Revelation 5:5**

He will forever be Jewish, and Satan cannot endure that the Last Adam is a Jew for all eternity.

So the prototype of the perfect man for all the people of the earth is a *Jewish Messiah*, a Jewish anointed King, possessor of all YHVH's authority! One that as a man was totally obedient to the Torah (see Matthew 28:18-20).

As a perfect Jewish man, King and High Priest, He is in heaven as the sole *mediator* between Father YHVH and all humans that choose to submit to Him.

> For there is one God and one Mediator between God and men, the (Jewish) Man Messiah Yeshua.
>
> — 1 Timothy 2:5

To sum it all up: The Messiah is a Jew, was born a Jew and will be a Jew for all eternity, only He will be a glorified Jew. A Jew died for you; a Jew intercedes for you, a Jew can be your lawyer in front of the judgment seat of the Almighty. (By the way, Jews make excellent lawyers.) Christians throughout the Ages were murdering Jews "in the name of Christ" because of Replacement Theology's deception that the "Jews killed Christ," and God is finished with them forever. But that *Antimesitojuz**, *Replacement Theology spirit, that lying murderous spirit, was getting even with the Jews because Yeshua is Jewish forever!*

So every time a Christian hates, depreciates, or kills Jews, it is the Messiah Yeshua Himself that they are killing.

Moreover, every time that a Christian rejects the very name of the Messiah Yeshua because His true name is Hebrew, meaning "salvation, healing, and deliverance," they are rejecting Salvation Himself.

YOU CANNOT HATE HIS TRUE NAME AND LOVE HIM!

Every time that they speak against the Jewish roots, the Torah, the Dietary Commandments or anything that they consider "Jewish" as expressed in the Bible – Holy Scriptures; it is the very Word of ELOHIM-God they are rejecting.

---

* Anti-messiah; Anti-Israel; Anti-Torah; Anti-Jewish; Anti-Zionist.

> *Rejecting, depreciating the Torah and any of ELOHIM's Commandments is rejecting Yeshua Himself.*
>
> *Yeshua is the Word (including the Torah) made flesh; He is the Word made into Jewish flesh to be more exact (John 1:14).*

Large portions of the Church need serious deliverance from the spirit of Anti-messiah:

> By this you know the Spirit of God: Every spirit that confesses that Yeshua the Messiah has come in the flesh (as a Jew) is of God, and every spirit that does not confess that Yeshua the Messiah has come in the flesh (as a Jew) is not of God.
>
> — 1 John 4:2-3

YESHUA IS YHVH'S HOLOGRAM

Another deception that has mostly plagued Jewish believers or Messianic believers is that Yeshua *is* the Son of God, *but* He is not God. This deception is born from the spirit of Anti-messiah as well, and it suits the Orthodox Jewish mindset that YHVH-God cannot be seen in the natural realm, that He is invisible; therefore Yeshua cannot possibly be YHVH.

> He is the image of the invisible God, the firstborn of all creation. For by Him all things were created, both in the heavens and on earth, visible and invisible, whether thrones or dominions or rulers or authorities— all things have been created through Him and for Him. He is before all things, and in Him all things hold together. He is also head of the body, the church; and He is the beginning, the firstborn from the dead, so that He Himself will come to have first place in everything. For it was the Father's good pleasure for all the fullness to dwell in Him, and through Him to reconcile all things to

Himself, having made peace through the blood of His cross; through Him, I say, whether things on earth or things in heaven.

— Colossians 1:15-20

Yeshua is the *mirror image* of the Father (YHVH); He is exactly like the Father except He can be visible in the natural realm and the Father is invisible. That is why He said, "If you see me you have seen the Father," He is the Father-YHVH in material/flesh form. In His pre-incarnate state the Father manifests Himself through Yeshua as the Captain of the Armies to Joshua and as the Angel of YHVH to Ya'akov and Samson's mother: (See Genesis 32:28; Joshua 5:14-15; Judges 13:18-22).

YESHUA IS THE "HOLOGRAM" OF THE FATHER

Holography (from the Greek ὅλος *hólos*, "whole" + γραφή *grafē*, "writing, drawing") is a technique which enables three-dimensional images to be made.

Yeshua is the whole word made flesh – the whole writing-hologram. (John 1:14)

> "If you had known Me, you would have known My Father also; and from now on you know Him and have seen Him."
>
> — John 14:7

Yeshua is *equal* with the Almighty and we must believe in Him like we believe in God:

> Let not your heart be troubled; you believe in God, believe also in Me.
>
> — John 14:1

Yeshua is worshiped by His Jewish Disciples while on earth.

> And Thomas answered and said to Him, "My Lᴏʀᴅ and my God!"
>
> — John 20:28

Yeshua is worshiped in heaven as the *visible* Lamb in the same manner that YHVH the Father is worshiped:

> And every creature which is in heaven and on the earth and under the earth and such as are in the sea, and all that are in them, I heard saying: "Blessing and honor and glory and power be to Him who sits on the throne, And to the Lamb, forever and ever!"
>
> — Revelation 5:13

You cannot separate between YHVH the Father and YHVH the Son; He is a mirror image of the Father like holograms are a mirror image of the thing or person that is being projected. In the same way that holograms have no life of their own, Yeshua has no life and no authority of His own because He is the absolute projection of YHVH, the Father. He is the visible form of the invisible God:

> He is the image of the invisible God, the firstborn of all creation.
>
> — Colossians 1:15

Yeshua and the Father are *one*:

> I and My Father are one.
>
> — John 10:30 NKJV

Shma (hear and obey) Israel, YHVH Eloheinu, YHVH *Echad* (is one).

> Hear, O Israel! YHVH is our Elohim, YHVH is one!
>
> — Deuteronomy 6:4

Yeshua being a type of hologram or mirror image of the invisible Elohim, is inseparable from Elohim, He is the Elohim that is visible.

YHVH the Father is invisible. YHVH the Son is visible.

> Yeshua said to him, "Have I been with you so long, and yet you have not known Me, Philip? He who has seen Me has seen the Father; so how can you say, 'Show us the Father'"?
>
> — John 14:9

They are *one* and the same, the same authority, the same power, the same character, the same attributes. Yeshua is submitted to YHVH the Father in the same way that your image in the mirror is submitted to *you*. Your image reflected in the mirror does not exist without *you*, but your image in the mirror is a projection of *you*!

> And the Word became flesh, and dwelt among us.
>
> — John 1:14a NKJV

Yeshua is the Firstborn of all creation on the one hand, and on the other hand, He created all things, so He created His own mirror image, His hologram because He is YHVH:

> He is the image of the invisible God, the firstborn of all creation. For by Him all things were created, both in the heavens and on earth,

visible and invisible, whether thrones or dominions or rulers or authorities— all things have been created through Him and for Him.

— Colossians 1:15-16 NKJV

THE MAGEN DAVID

There are many teachings out there that label the Star of David, the Jewish National emblem in the flag of Israel as demonic. Satan is truly afraid of what this emblem means, so he stirs up more anti-Jewish feelings through the hatred of the Star or rather the Shield of David. New Age has used many symbols such as the Cross, but interestingly enough there are almost no teachings against the symbol of the Cross being demonic, though it has been used in the occult numerous times. Satan tends to use everything holy and pervert it. He is an imitator and not a Creator! That is why he takes music created by ELOHIM and perverts it. He takes all the *omanut* (arts) and perverts them. Does that mean that *all* music is of Satan and or dancing, or theater or painting? Of course not. YHVH is the Creator, and He has given humankind His own creativity:

> Then ELOHIM said, "Let Us make man in Our image, according to Our likeness; and let them rule over the fish of the sea and over the birds of the sky and over the cattle and over all the earth, and over every creeping thing that creeps on the earth." God created man in His own image, in the image of God He created him; male and female He created them.
>
> — Genesis 1:26-27

THE MAGEN DAVID (SHIELD OF DAVID, NOT STAR) IS A TREMENDOUSLY PROPHETIC SYMBOL

The two triangles represent both the humanity and divinity of the Messiah. One triangle points down, describing ELOHIM coming down to man's level and the other triangle points up, which represents man coming up to ELOHIM. Triangles have three parts representing the Tri-unity of ELOHIM being Father, Son, and Holy Spirit, inseparable and indivisible (not *Trinity* which means three separate gods as a Greek deception but *Tri-unity; One—Echad* in plurality).

> He is the image of the invisible God, the firstborn of all creation. For by Him all things were created, both in the heavens and on earth, visible and invisible, whether thrones or dominions or rulers or authorities— all things have been created through Him and for Him.
> — Colossians 1:15-16

THE GOD TRIANGLE POINTING DOWN

The God triangle of the Shield of David, which is pointing down, represents the Tri-unity of ELOHIM coming down to man in the form of Messiah Yeshua, YHVH the Son!

> In the beginning was the Word, and the Word was with God, and the Word was God. He was in the beginning with God. All things came into being through Him, and apart from Him nothing came into being that has come into being. And the Word became flesh, and dwelt among us, and we saw His glory, glory as of the only begotten from the Father, full of grace and truth.
> — John 1:1-3,14 NKJV

The human triangle which points up has three parts representing Adam and all mankind created in the image and likeness of the Creator. Human beings are also triune beings like ELOHIM. Humans are a spirit being, they have a soul, and they live in a body.

> Now may the God of peace Himself sanctify you entirely; and may your spirit and soul and body be preserved complete, without blame at the coming of our LORD Yeshua the Messiah.
> — 1 Thessalonians 5:23 NKJV

For all eternity redeemed human beings will be a spirit being, will have a soul and will live in a glorified body. That is why the resurrection from the dead is in *bodily* form! All three parts of man are essential just like the Tri-unity of ELOHIM is. When Yeshua rose from the dead, He rose in a glorified body and the marks of the nails was still in His glorified hands. (By the way, so was the mark of the circumcision – that is why He is called in heaven a Jewish Lion or the Lion of Judah. See Revelation 5:5.)

> So also is the resurrection of the dead the body is sown in corruption, it is raised in incorruption. It is sown in dishonor, it is raised in glory. It is sown in weakness, it is raised in power. It is sown a natural body, it is raised a spiritual body.
> — 1 Corinthians 15:42-44

The two triangles of the Magen David represent all divinity and all humanity coming together in Yeshua the Messiah, the Son of David.

Once we accept Yeshua in His fullness as being YHVH manifested in Jewish flesh—all God and all man—it is a *shield* to our faith and mind!

May the revelation of the Magen David be imprinted in your mind as you accept Yeshua as *both* God-YHVH-Elohim and a Jewish man – the Last Adam. And may the Magen David printed on the flag of Israel be revealed soon to all our Jewish people that they may believe in Him, Messiah Yeshua, who is the visible image, the hologram of YHVH the invisible Elohim:

> Who, although He existed in the form of God, did not regard equality with God a thing to be grasped, but emptied Himself, taking the form of a bond-servant, and being made in the likeness of men. Being found in appearance as a man, He humbled Himself by becoming obedient to the point of death, even death on a cross. For this reason also, God highly exalted Him, and bestowed on Him the name which is above every name, so that at the name of Yeshua every knee will bow, of those who are in heaven and on earth and under the earth, and that every tongue will confess that Yeshua HaMashiach is Lord (Adonai, YHVH, the Ultimate Ruler), to the glory of YHVH-Elohim-God the Father.
>
> – Philippians 2:6-11 NKJV

And as the Prophet Isaiah so eloquently puts the divinity and humanity of Yeshua, the Son that is born:

> For a child will be born to us, a son will be given to us; and the government will rest on His shoulders; and His name will be called Wonderful Counselor, Mighty God, Eternal Father, Prince of Peace. There will be no end to the increase of His government or of peace,

on the throne of David and over his kingdom, to establish it and to uphold it with justice and righteousness from then on and forevermore. The zeal of YHVH of hosts will accomplish this.

— Isaiah 9:5-7

This child that was born 2,000 years ago as a Jew whose name is Yeshua, meaning "salvation," is also Mighty God and Eternal Father – He is YHVH.

The zeal of YHVH has indeed accomplished these 2,000 years ago, and Yeshua is soon to return and plant His feet on the Mount of Olives to rule and reign from Jerusalem over all nations of the earth.

CHAPTER 14

COMMON DEADLY DECEPTIONS

> Get rid of the old yeast, so that you may be a new unleavened batch—as you really are. For Messiah, our Passover lamb has been sacrificed.
>
> — *1 Corinthians 5:7*

WE ARE SOON celebrating Passover and the Feast of *Matzo* (Unleavened Bread). This time is a powerful season of cleansing and deliverance, remembering Israel's miraculous exodus from Egypt and removing all leaven (sin) out of our lives. Yeshua is the ultimate Passover Lamb that rescues us from the Egypt of sin that brings death! Paul admonishes us to keep the Feast of Passover which is the first feast of the Holy Biblical Celebration cycle described in Leviticus 23:

> **Therefore let us keep the Festival, not with the old bread leavened with malice and wickedness, but with the unleavened bread of sincerity and truth.**
>
> — 1 Corinthians 5:8

Too many people are "good Christians" trying to do the best they can for the LORD and yet are perishing because of what I would call common yet very deadly deceptions. These deceptions look good and feel good, but they are snakes in disguise. We must understand that the best way that Satan can win over us is through lies and deceptions. He knows that if he would come against God-fearing people with horns on and a horrible winnowing fork he will have no customers among the Church goers. He must find a way to poison us that will look acceptable and even palatable, so the deception must be mixed with something that is morally or socially "good" in essence or at least not too harmful.

> **No wonder, for even Satan disguises himself as an angel of light.**
>
> — 2 Corinthians 11:14

I will mention here a few of these deceptions that I have found all over the world. Notice your reaction when you read about them. The devil does not like to lose territory easily, so the spirits that have been "cozy" in your life may react with great upset when exposed to the light! If you find that you get upset with me, really surprised or "ticked off" by the contents of this message, you have fallen prey of these common deadly deceptions already and need *repentance* and *deliverance*.

Remember that the snake in the Garden of Eden tempted the woman and the man to believe that ELOHIM was not so good because He forbade them to eat the fruit of such a "pleasant tree" as the Tree of Knowledge of Good and Evil.

> **When the woman saw that the tree was good for food, and that it was a delight to the eyes, and that the tree was desirable to make one wise, she took from its fruit and ate; and she gave also to her husband with her, and he ate.**
>
> — Genesis 3:6

Deceptions usually are "nice," "pleasant" and "good for you," but, "the good is always the enemy of the perfect." I remember that before I was saved, I delved into New Age practices such as Yoga, meditation and Occult. The "spirit guides" that I inquired of used to convince me that smoking strong cigarettes was good for me as it helped me to be more "spiritual." This was over 23 years ago before the aggressive campaign against cigarette smoking started; of course now any intelligent person knows that cigarettes can be deadly. But this is the nature of deception. It is an attack on our conscience and God-given intelligence. The first thing that Yeshua took away from me by the power of His Holy Spirit was cigarette smoking. It was killing me both naturally and spiritually! And yes, there is both a natural and a spiritual side to all common and deadly deceptions:

> **However, the spiritual is not first, but the natural; then the spiritual.**
>
> — 1 Corinthians 15:46

Please read on, and at the end I will lead you in a prayer of repentance and deliverance so you can be set *free*.

YOGA, MEDITATION, AND MARTIAL ARTS

One of the most common and deadly deceptions of our times is the practice of *Yoga*. This particular *religion* has invaded our public schools, kinder-gardens, and nearly all health care even for babies. The lie that Satan has sold to this generation is that Yoga is a natural, physical practice that helps your body be fit, and your mind be *calm*. Since we are living in terribly noisy and stressful times, Yoga has a lot of "customers" even among Christians and Messianic believers. But what is *yoga* and where is its origin? Remember the principle of Matthew 7:

> "Watch out for false prophets. They come to you in sheep's clothing, but inwardly they are ferocious wolves. By their fruit you will recognize them. Do people pick grapes from thorn bushes, or figs from thistles? Likewise, every good tree bears good fruit, but a bad tree bears bad fruit. A good tree cannot bear bad fruit, and a bad tree cannot bear good fruit.
> — Matthew 7:15-18

This principle should accompany us in testing everything. What is the *root* of Yoga? If we know the root or seed, we will know which tree is it. The Tree of Knowledge of Good and Evil, or the Tree of Life.

> And YHVH Elohim commanded the man, "You are free to eat from any tree in the garden; but you must not eat from the tree of the

knowledge of good and evil, for when you eat from it you will certainly die.

— Genesis 2:16-17

The origins of Yoga are in India:

Yoga (Sanskrit, Pāli: योग yóga) refers to traditional physical, mental, and spiritual disciplines, originating in India, whose goal is the attainment of a state of perfect spiritual insight and tranquility. The word is associated with meditative practices in Hinduism, Buddhism and Jainism. (Feuerstein, Oxford University Press)

Yoga has a *Guru* or Master that all those who practice Yoga are bound to whether they know it or not. The physical practices are not just innocent exercises to help your body and nervous mind. They are powerful "katas" or spiritual dance and meditation movements that invoke the spirits of Occult and New Age and that connect you with the "Master Mind" (Satan) body language is well known to be more powerful than words sometimes, and so it is with Yoga. While you are innocently doing the "lotus position" and "Mantras" (repetition of certain words like "OM") you are communicating... When you are doing the "tiger position" you are communicating... Those demon spirits make their home in you because you have called them:

> The essence of Guru Yoga is simply to remember the guru at all times: when you are happy, think of the guru; when you are sad, think of the guru; when you meet favorable circumstances, be grateful to the guru;

and when you meet obstacles, pray to the guru, and rely on him alone. When you are sitting, think of the guru above your head. When you are walking, imagine that he is above your right shoulder, as if you were circumambulating him. When you are eating food, visualize the guru at your throat center and offer him the first portion. Whenever you wear new clothes, first offer them to the guru, and then wear them as if he had given them back to you.

At night, when you are about to fall asleep, visualize Guru Rinpoche in your heart center. (Reversespins.com)

SPIRITUAL MOVEMENTS

Movement is such a powerful force that the Spirit of YHVH is depicted as a Female Dancer in the Book of Genesis, that floats and dances over the face of the abyss bringing wholeness to the chaotic earth.

> **The earth was without form and an empty waste, and darkness was upon the face of the very great deep. The Spirit of God was moving (hovering, brooding) over the face of the waters.**
>
> **— Genesis 1:2**

Satan is an imitator and the Father of Lies, thus he is always imitating what is pure, holy and powerful with his demonic version.

Movement and dance is a very spiritual thing, and so is all exercise. We can be inhabited by the Holy Spirit or by demon spirits when we move, exercise and dance. All the "Martial

Arts" such as Kung-Fu and Karate are connected to a "Master Mind" through spiritual exercises and invoke demonic spirits in the guise of "physical exercise."

> Yoga, religious meditation and martial arts have evil origins in eastern practices of Hinduism, Buddhism, Taoism and Zen which are based on occultism. Transcendental meditation (blanking out and emptying the mind) is the spiritual root system and foundation of martial arts, yoga and related arts. People worship many deities; Pantheism is the toleration of worship of all gods, the view that everything is GOD and the belief that man is GOD. Evil spirits of martial arts are warrior spirits, dragon spirits, snake spirits, animal spirits, spirit of Kundaline, spirit guides, etc. exhibiting power, rage and violence. There is idol worship of the gurus and senseis (teachers). Inner consciousness movement is mind control from cosmic demonic power. These are philosophies, practices and spiritual experiences. (Demonbuster.com)

People and even believers that delve into these practices are worshiping another god with their movements, even in their ignorance. The body language that they use invokes other "gods" (demon spirits) who gladly come to destroy your relationship with YHVH! The Scripture is evident in the *first* of the Ten Commandments:

> You shall not bow down to them or serve them; for I, the Lord your God, am a jealous God, visiting the iniquity of the fathers upon the children to the third and fourth generations of those who hate Me.
> — Deuteronomy 5:7-9

What is the purpose of our movements? Who do we dance for? All movement is a form of worship, that is why the Word says to love the LORD with all our strength as well as heart and mind. All the eastern martial arts and spiritual/physical practices include movements of *worship*; except they are not directed towards the Living God. They are instead designed for the worship of "other gods" though most people are not aware of it.

If we need to achieve tranquility and peace, Yeshua has sent us His Holy Spirit. When we are baptized in the Holy Spirit, He gives us a heavenly language called "Tongues." When we pray in Tongues and worship the Father in Spirit and Truth we can rest as we pray through. It is amazing how many Christians have rejected the Baptism in the Holy Spirit which includes praying/worshiping in heavenly languages and yet they have accepted Yoga, Meditation and Martial Arts which are satanic religions!

Praying in Tongues is also called "praying in the Holy Spirit," and it builds up our faith which brings peace of mind:

> But you, beloved, building yourselves up on your most holy faith, praying in the Holy Spirit.
> — Jude 20

When we meditate on the Word day and night (Joshua 1:8), we receive revelation, and that brings peace to our souls. When we need to express physically, we can sing and dance to Him.

"Let everything that has breath praise YHVH!"

— Psalms 150:6

A PRAYER OF DELIVERANCE

Please pray this powerful prayer to be free of the deadly deception of Yoga and all Martial Arts, even if you did it in the past.

> Father in heaven, I confess the worship of other gods in the form of Yoga, Meditation, Kung Fu, Tai Chi, and Karate (name the one that fits you). I ask your forgiveness for my ignorance and here and now renounce these practices and all its spiritual and physical implications. I break the power of the spirits involved in them and any ungodly soul ties I may have developed with any masters or teachers of them or any gurus. I commit myself to destroy and burn all clothing or other artifacts connected with Yoga and Martial Arts. I will have no traces of them in my life, not even as "souvenirs!" in Yeshua's name!

> Father, thank you that the Blood of Yeshua cleanses me from all sin and sets me free from all unrighteousness! I am *free* to worship only *You* in Spirit and Truth. You are the source of my Peace and tranquility. Please fill

me with Your Holy Spirit and give me Your heavenly Languages to worship you in Spirit and Truth in Yeshua's name. Amen!

And you will know the truth, and the truth will make you free.
— John 8:32

ONCE SAVED ALWAYS SAVED

Little children, make sure no one deceives you; the one who practices righteousness is righteous, just as He is righteous; the one who practices sin is of the devil.
— 1 John 3:7-8

One of the most common deadly deceptions is the "once saved, always saved" doctrine. I believe that this particular doctrine has killed too many people!

In fact, some Christians and some religious Jews harbor the same dangerous belief that *choice* has nothing to do with salvation. In other words it is all predestined and we humans have no say. Among many Orthodox Jews the theory is: "No matter how much we sin, we cannot lose our 'Jewish Soul'. Immorality, homosexuality and the like cannot make us lose our 'Jewish Soul.'" However, they say believing in Yeshua is the only thing that can cause us to lose this precious soul. That is why when many of us Jews accept Messiah; our closest family sits *shiva* for us (which means they do a ceremony of mourning for the dead) and sit in desolation and grief for seven days on the floor as if we died.

Among the Christians, something very similar happens when many believe that it does not matter what a Christian does as long as he "believes" in Jesus—that belief with no need for *repentance* or *cleansing* is enough to "go to heaven" and inherit Eternal Life. In the case of the Christian deception there is only one thing that can cause a Christian to lose their salvation, and that is *Judaizing* or most particularly following anything Jewish. They often quote from Galatians 3-5 about this very misunderstood subject. The persecution against a person that desires to enjoy the Jewish Messiah in His Jewish context is fierce, to say the least.

Both Christians and Jews share common deceptions. This connection shows in a peculiar way how tied are the Christians and the Jews and how much we belong together!

The Word of God is evident that not everyone who considers himself a Jew is saved. Both Jews and Gentiles need to *repent* and receive forgiveness of sins.

Two thousand years ago, only Jews could be saved; only Jews had a Covenant with the Almighty God. Paul made a point in the Book of Romans that ethnicity (being ethnically Jew by birth) is not enough for salvation.

> A person is not a Jew who is one only outwardly, nor is circumcision merely outward and physical. No, a person is a Jew who is one inwardly; and circumcision is circumcision of the heart, by the Spirit, not by the written code. Such a person's praise is not from other people, but from God.
>
> — Romans 2:28-29

This passage is very revealing as we could now change it and say, "a person is not a Christian who is one only outwardly, nor is circumcision merely outward and physical." No, a person is a Christian who is one inwardly; and circumcision is circumcision of the heart, by the Spirit, not by the written code. Such a person's praise is not from other people but from God.

Paul said that the *circumcision* of the *heart* was needed. In other words, the *flesh* or the *carnality* of the heart needed to be *removed* so that YHVH could write His Commandments and ways there!

There is a *big* difference in the nature between a man that is circumcised and a man that is not, it is *noticeable*. In the same way there is a big difference between a believer in Yeshua that is circumcised of heart and one that is religious and shows no change of heart and lifestyle.

Yeshua warned us against the belief that Salvation meant only to believe that Yeshua died for our sins and that no *repentance* is needed. He informed us that a true believer would also be an *obedient* person. He clearly said that the disobedient "believers" would not be saved. He called those "believers" that disobey Him *evildoers* or wicked people that are *lawless*. In other words, their hearts had not been circumcised, and the Commandments of the Most High are not written in there:

> "Not everyone who says to Me, 'Lord, Lord,' will enter the kingdom of heaven, but only the one who does the will of My Father who is in heaven. Many will say to Me on that day, 'Lord, Lord, did we not prophesy in Your name and in Your name drive out demons and in

Your name perform many miracles?' Then I will tell them plainly, 'I never knew you. Away from me, you evildoers!'

— Matthew 7:21-23

He clearly said that "believers" who walk in the futility of their minds, keep on sinning, and are carnal are regarded as His enemies and die eternally:

For if you are living according to the flesh, you must die; but if by the Spirit you are putting to death the deeds of the body, you will live.

— Romans 8:13

If you know that He is righteous, you know that everyone also who practices righteousness is born of Him.

— 1 John 2:29

Little children, make sure no one deceives you; the one who practices righteousness is righteous, just as He is righteous; the one who practices sin is of the devil; for the devil has sinned from the beginning The Son of God appeared for this purpose, to destroy the works of the devil.

— 1 John 3:7-8

THE FULL PROGRESSION OF SALVATION

In the Book of Leviticus chapter 16, we have a most revealing progression of *salvation*. During the holiest day of the Biblical Calendar, the Day of Atonement or *Yom HaKipurim*, the High Priest needed to take some radical steps to bring yearly salvation to all of Israel. These steps are very revealing of the process of *redemption*.

> **For it is on this day that atonement shall be made for you to cleanse you; you will be clean from all your sins before YHVH.**
> **— Leviticus 16:30**

It included the blood of a sacrificed goat as a sin offering to atone for the sins of Israel, and another goat, called a "scapegoat" on whose head the High Priest *confessed* the sins of Israel and then sent it carrying the sins to the wilderness. Then the High Priest needed to *wash*, *dress* in His priestly garments, and finally he had to offer the *burnt offering*.

In the same manner, Yeshua became that goat for *sin*, and His blood brought about forgiveness of sin (Ephesians 1:7). He is also the scapegoat that *removes* our sin. So, following *forgiveness* (Blood) comes *sin removal* (Confession: 1 John 1:9). Once we have been forgiven, and our sins confessed and removed; now we need to wash with the water of the Word (that means meditating in the Word day and night) to remove any dirt left by sin (Ephesians 5:26). Following the washing we must dress in the New Man in our new Royal Priesthood garments (Ephesians 4:24; 1 Peter 2:9) so we can offer our own flesh as a burnt offering before YHVH! We must become the High Priest of our own body and offer it as a Living Sacrifice to ELOHIM-God, in other words to *live* for Him alone!

THE WONDERFUL SMELL OF BURNING FLESH

> Therefore I urge you, brethren, by the mercies of God, to present your bodies a living and holy sacrifice, acceptable to God, which is your spiritual service of worship.
> — Romans 12:1

When your flesh burns, you will obey God in all that He asks you to do, including in your *giving*. Paul called the act of sacrificial giving a "sweet-smelling aroma" like in the case of the burnt offerings in the Holy Temple in Jerusalem and from the beginning of time (Genesis 4:4-5).

> But I have received everything in full and have an abundance; I am amply supplied, having received from Epaphroditus what you have sent, a fragrant aroma, an acceptable sacrifice, well-pleasing to God.
> — Philippians 4:18

True salvation will affect our lives in *every* way. The way we live will radically *change* to match the Biblical culture. If there is no change, no *repentance*, no *obedience* to His Holy Spirit and Word, the Blood of Yeshua cannot help us anymore:

> For if we go on sinning willfully after receiving the knowledge of the truth, there no longer remains a sacrifice for sins, but a terrifying expectation of judgment and the fury of a fire which will consume the adversaries. Anyone who has set aside the Law of Moses dies without mercy on the testimony of two or three witnesses. How much severer punishment do you think he will deserve who has trampled underfoot the Son of God, and has regarded as unclean

the blood of the covenant by which he was sanctified, and has insulted the Spirit of grace?

— Hebrews 10:26-29

True salvation will lead us to true deliverance from sin and to radical obedience in every area of our lives, including our body, mind, attitudes, and *finances*. The smell of burnt flesh in every area of our lives will be pleasing unto YHVH:

'So because you are lukewarm, and neither hot nor cold, I will spit you out of My mouth.

— Revelation 3:16

If we are *hot*, the flesh will *burn* and we will smell good to the LORD.

The only way that we can keep on smelling good and on the narrow road of Salvation is to be filled with His Holy Spirit's Fire and not to quench it with sin and disobedience, with murmuring, complaining, and unbelief. Paul said that he worked his salvation with fear and trembling because he did not believe in the deceptive doctrine of "once saved, always saved." He knew that we needed to walk a radical walk of obedience and holiness every single day:

So then, my beloved, just as you have always obeyed, not as in my presence only, but now much more in my absence, work out your salvation with fear and trembling.

— Philippians 2:12

First, we must receive the Baptism of the Holy Spirit and Fire and then we must learn to feed the *fire* with obedient acts of faith in every area of our lives.

The Gospel and the Torah (the Word of God) must affect all areas of our lives. Our obedience to walk in holiness does not depend on any circumstances but on Him who calls. We have an *eternity* to enjoy the choices that we made in *this* life! (note: The Bible says that we live only once, and afterward the judgment happens. Reincarnation is another common and deadly deception.)

Many of those who sleep in the dust of the ground will awake, these to everlasting life, but the others to disgrace and everlasting contempt.
— Daniel 12:2

A LIFE-CHANGING PRAYER

I say *yes Adon* (LORD) Yeshua (the actual name of Jesus), come and save me to the uttermost! I give my life entirely to You. I ask forgiveness from all my sins and rebellion, and I receive it. I am yours forever! Pour out Your Holy Spirit and Fire and make me burn for You! *Amen.*

CHAPTER 15

FLEE THE KABBALAH DECEPTION

> And no wonder, for Satan himself masquerades as an angel of light.
>
> — *2 Corinthians 11:14*

A WHILE AGO, WE were invited to minister in Ecuador to a congregation that has chosen to network with our ministry as we mentor them. As I was ministering to the people after a touching teaching calling to repentance from various things, some of the members asked for prayer.

They said to me, "Some time ago, Messianic Rabbi G. from another town came and taught us about the 'Jewish roots,' including some things about Kabbalah, Sefirot or emanations. He laid hands on us and 'blessed' us. Since he blessed us we cannot hear the voice of the Holy Spirit. We feel strange and oppressed!"

I immediately asked them to repent from listening to deceptive theologies and for letting this particular "Rabbi" laid hands on them. As they did, I broke the curse of Kabbalah, cast out the spirit of deception and New Age and declared the power of Yeshua's Blood to deliver. Immediately these people fell under the power of God and came back restored to their relationship with Yeshua like babies, ready to drink the pure milk of the Word. The oppression left, and the anointing returned. HaleluYah!

JUDAISM VS. TORAH

One of the most common deceptions among Christians returning to the Jewish roots of the faith is the entanglement with unbiblical "Jewish" traditions and especially the Kabbalah and the Talmud. It is imperative that we understand that not everything "Jewish" is also "Hebrew" or Biblical. *Judaism is a religious system, much like Christianity that its source is in the poisonous tree of Knowledge of Good and Evil.*

> **The YHVH Elohim commanded the man, saying, "From any tree of the garden you may eat freely; but from the tree of the knowledge of good and evil you shall not eat, for in the day that you eat from it you will surely die."**
>
> **— Genesis 2:16-17**

When we call people to return to the Jewish roots, Hebrew foundations of the Gospel, the call is not to another religious system but to the truth of the Hebrew Holy Scriptures, namely the *Tanakh* as in its entirety: Both the "Old" Testament and New Testament is the Word of ELOHIM-God:

> **Thus says YHVH, "Stand by the ways and see and ask for the ancient paths, where the good way is, and walk in it; and you will find rest for your souls.**
>
> **— Jeremiah 6:16**

When we call the people to forsake feasts of pagan origin such as Christmas, Easter, and Halloween and restore the Holy *Moadim*—feasts and convocations—*we are not calling people to Judaism but Torah.* The Torah is described in the First Five Books of the Bible as the instructions given to the people of Israel. Yeshua spoke highly of the Torah when He emphatically said that He did not come to abolish it:

> **"Do not think that I came to abolish the Law or the Prophets; I did not come to abolish but to fulfill. For truly I say to you, until heaven and earth pass away, not the smallest letter or stroke shall pass from the Law until all is accomplished. Whoever then annuls one of the least of these commandments, and teaches others to do the same, shall be called least in the kingdom of heaven; but whoever keeps and teaches them, he shall be called great in the kingdom of heaven.**
>
> **— Matthew 5:17-19**

In other words, Yeshua through the Holy Spirit is the one that interprets the Torah to His followers. Not any other Jewish Rabbi or theologian, not the Talmud, Kabbalah, or any external book to the Bible! It is important to note that we can only walk in obedience to YHVH's Commandments when we are born again, spirit-filled, and live in intimate communion with Yeshua the Jewish Messiah. Any attempts to "be good" without His Perfect Blood Atonement is totally futile and leads to religiosity and to fall from grace:

> And Yeshua said to him, "Why do you call Me good? No one is good except God alone.
>
> — Luke 18:19

> Yeshua answered, "Truly, truly, I say to you, unless one is born of water and the Spirit he cannot enter into the kingdom of God. That which is born of the flesh is flesh, and that which is born of the Spirit is spirit.
>
> — John 3:5-6

The Torah written in the hearts and minds of the New Covenant believers is the only Biblical sign that they are indeed in the New Covenant. Only the Holy Spirit can write the Torah in our hearts.

> "Behold, days are coming," declares YHVH, "when I will make a new covenant with the house of Israel and with the house of Judah, not like the covenant which I made with their fathers in the day I took them by the hand to bring them out of the land of Egypt, My covenant which they broke, although I was a husband to them," declares the Lord. "But this is the covenant which I will make with the house of Israel after those days," declares the Lord, "I will put My law (Torah) within them and on their heart I will write it; and I will be their God, and they shall be My people.
>
> — Jeremiah 31:31-34

Please note that the New Covenant is made with the House of Israel and Judah and not with the Gentiles. Gentiles join into a preexisting New Covenant with the Ancient and Chosen (forever) people of Israel through the royal, holy Blood of the Jewish Messiah Yeshua.

> Therefore remember that formerly you, the Gentiles in the flesh, who are called "Uncircumcision" by the so-called "Circumcision," which is performed in the flesh by human hands. Remember that you were at that time separate from Messiah, excluded from the commonwealth of Israel, and strangers to the covenants of promise, having no hope and without God in the world. But now in Messiah Yeshua you who formerly were far off have been brought near by the blood of Messiah.
> — Ephesians 2:11-13

There is no New Covenant without Israel and Judah, and there is no other Messiah besides Yeshua the Jewish Messiah, the Word of God made flesh, the Son of ELOHIM who left His divinity to become a man fulfilling numerous prophecies:

> For a child will be born to us, a son will be given to us; And the government will rest on His shoulders; and His name will be called Wonderful Counselor, Mighty God, Eternal Father, Prince of Peace.
> — Isaiah 9:6

TORAH IS HOLY, NOT JUDAISM

> Your word, YHVH, is eternal; it stands firm in the heavens.
> — Psalms 119:89

As I stated before, Judaism is not our goal when we return to the Jewish/Hebrew foundations of faith or what I call "The Gospel made in Zion." While there are some Jewish traditions that are very beautiful and even prophetic, there are others that are purely heretical. Kabbalah is a religious system within Judaism that is born of Satan (who disguises himself as an angel of light) to deceive the Jews even further. It is a Replacement Theology system that seeks to replace the work of the Ruach Hakodesh (Holy Spirit), the truth of Yeshua and the New Covenant. It is born during the Middle Ages in France and moves to Spain. That says a lot about the source of Kabbalah, as the Middle Ages are also called the "Dark Ages." It was a time so dark in the history of humanity that it gave birth to many religious heresies.

> Watch out for false prophets. They come to you in sheep's clothing, but inwardly they are ferocious wolves. By their fruit you will recognize them. Do people pick grapes from thorn-bushes, or figs from thistles? Likewise, every good tree bears good fruit, but a bad tree bears bad fruit.
>
> — Matthew 7:15-17

Today Kabbalah is regarded as "Torah" by many and even more important than the Torah received by Moses. To make it "valid" Kabbalists state that Moses got the Kabbalah when he went up Mount Sinai for the second time! Their statements are totally opposed by the Hebrew Holy Scriptures that state that both on the first and the second time, Moses got the Tablets of the Testimony from YHVH (Ten Commandments). *There is no mention in the Holy Scriptures about the Kabbalah at all.*

> And he hewed two tables of stone like unto the first; and Moses rose up early in the morning, and went up unto Mount Sinai, as YHVH had commanded him, and took in his hand two tables of stone.
> — Exodus 34:4

The *Kabbalah* (Hebrew for "handed down by tradition") made its appearance in the twelfth Century in Provence, southern France, which at the time was the scene of the Cathar heresy (one of several dualistic religious revivals during the Middle Ages). It reached maturity, however, in thirteenth-Century Spain, with the composition of *Sefer haZohar* ("The Book of Splendor"). Henceforth, the Kabbalah became the primary trend of Jewish mysticism, theosophy, and esotericism, comprising many different, at times contradictory, approaches.

Kabbalists wanted to transform Judaism into a more profound inner experience; an experience, so they believed, that could not be attained through a rational and intellectual approach to religion. For them Judaism was a system of mystical symbols reflecting the mystery of God and the universe, and they aimed to discover keys to the understanding of this symbolism.

The *Zohar*, generally attributed to Moses de Leon, sought to revive a "communion" between the faithful and divinity. The Divine manifests itself in ten *Sefirot* (emanations) representing an intermediate stage between God and creation. Just as these emanations are contained within the Godhead, so they impregnate all beings outside it. Man is capable, by practicing precise rites, of influencing the *Sefirot* which determine the span and progress of the world. The theory of *Sefirot* became the backbone of Spanish kabbalist teachings, represented by a great number of images.

In time, two attitudes emerged: one esoteric, which tried to restrict the secrets of kabbalist wisdom to a small circle of initiates; and a second which insisted that it should be widelyspread, benefiting everyone. (Barnavi)

Kabbalists refer to the Mosaic encounters as the outer and inner teaching. The first encounter of Moses with God is when he received the 10 Commandments. This is called the outer teaching. *It was upon the second encounter with God that Moses received the Kabbalistic truths. This is referred to as the inner teaching.*

Throughout history, Kabbalists have chosen to keep their esoteric interpretations of the Torah hidden from the general populace and religious leaders of the day. *Many of the Kabbalists were persecuted and many others knew that their teachings contradicted accepted Jewish and Christian theologies. Therefore, they practiced a self-imposed silence.*

Today Kabbalah has become popularized by such writers as Yehuda Berg and spread by the internet and TV. Many traditional Jewish cabalists condemn contemporary Kabbalah movements as fanciful and overly popularized misrepresentations of authentic Kabbalistic philosophy. *Whichever the case, today's Kabbalah is definitely more new age than biblical. Even though modern popularized Kabbalah has been condemned by traditional cabalists, readings from the Zohar, which is several hundred years old and is at the heart of Kabbalah, reveals theology reminiscent of the new age: reincarnation, inner divinity, pantheism, etc.*

The truth is that Kabbalah has evolved. But it has evolved from one heresy deeper into another. It is not biblical and it is not true. (Carm.org)

Yehuda Ashlag's textbook *Talmud Eser Sefirot (the Study of the Ten Sefirot)* is designed as a study aid with questions, answers, materials for repetition and explanations. This is, if you will, the physics of the upper worlds, describing the laws and forces governing the universe on the spiritual realm.

This material gradually transforms the students, because when searching how to experience the spiritual world, one gradually adapts oneself to the spiritual laws described in the textbook.

The science of Kabbalah does not deal with life in this world. *Instead, by studying this system we re-attain the level we possessed before we descended. During this ascent, the study of Kabbalah builds within the student a system equal to the spiritual system.* (Kabbalah.info)

The Word of ELOHIM tells us that there is only one *Mediator* between God and man; Yeshua the Messiah, certainly no "emanations" or "*Sefirot*":

> For there is one God and one mediator between God and mankind, the man Messiah Yeshua.
>
> — 1 Timothy 2:5

Also, the Word of God-ELOHIM tells us that we cannot "improve ourselves" by studying anything to be restored to relationship with the Creator. We must repent of our sins and accept the only blood atonement that releases Yah's (God's) forgiveness towards us – the Blood of Yeshua." We must be born again; we cannot "evolve."

> Yeshua replied, "Very truly I tell you, no one can see the kingdom of God unless they are born again.
>
> — John 3:3

Kabbalah is looking to help men "ascend" to the Almighty and to become "divine" much like the Tower of Babel.

> Then they said, "Come, let us build ourselves a city, with a tower that reaches to the heavens, so that we may make a name for ourselves; otherwise we will be scattered over the face of the whole earth."
>
> — Genesis 11:4

The Word of God tells us that all our works are like filthy rags:

> But we are all as an unclean thing, and all our righteousnesses are as filthy rags (menstrual cloths!); and we all do fade as a leaf; and our iniquities, like the wind, have taken us away.
>
> — Isaiah 64:6

We must repent, be forgiven, and be born again. The Bible tells us that the heart is desperately wicked:

> The heart is deceitful above all things, and desperately wicked: who can know it?
>
> — Jeremiah 17:9

We cannot "improve" the condition of our hearts with any study; we must get a *new heart*:

> I will give you a new heart and put a new spirit in you; I will remove from you your heart of stone and give you a heart of flesh.
>
> — Ezekiel 36:26

In short, Kabbalah is the most popular form of "Jewish" New Age with much Hinduism (reincarnation), and it denies the need for repentance from sin and blood atonement.

> For the life of a creature is in the blood, and I have given it to you to make atonement for yourselves on the altar; it is the blood that makes atonement for one's life.
>
> — Leviticus 17:10

Thus it is not "Jewish" at all but rather pagan and New Age Those who practice Kabbalah will suffer demon oppression, possession, will hear voices of dead Rabbis as "ascended masters" and "spiritual guides," will be in great confusion and can also be affected by spiritual madness and mental sickness.

> **My sheep hear my voice, and I know them, and they follow me.**
> **— John 10:27**

Because Kabbalah is "another gospel" and another "Torah," it will bring many curses and will cause those Messianic or Christian believers delving into it to fall from Grace. The anointing of the Holy Spirit will leave such a person, and evil spirits of New Age will take His place:

> **But even if we or an angel from heaven should preach to you a gospel contrary to and different from that which we preached to you, let him be accursed (anathema, devoted to destruction, doomed to eternal punishment)!**
> **— Galatians 1:8 Amplified Bible**

If you have fallen prey to this deception, please go on your knees *today*, repent and renounce it and command the spirits of Kabbalah and New Age to leave your life for good in Yeshua's name! Immerse yourself in the Holy Scriptures and burn all deceptive books in your possession! I strongly suggest that you order our books *Eradicating the Cancer of Religion* and *Grafted In* to help you in your deliverance and quest for the true Jewish roots of the Gospel. Order from www.kadesh.org – Press on "Shop." You can also join our Israeli Bible School, GRM, so you can be well rooted and ready for Endtime service.[*]

---

[*] https://www.grmbibleschool.com/

CHAPTER 16

REMOVING FALSE ASSUMPTIONS

"Love thinks no evil."

— *1 Corinthians 13:5 NKJV*

---

*L*ATELY, I HAVE been noticing how many relationships in life go sour because of mistaken assumptions; countless amounts of strife and broken relationships happen because of incorrect assumptions among them: Strained relationships between parents and children; husband and wives; pastors and their flocks; and simple friends. Without this wicked attitude of the heart and mind, it would be easy to have loving and harmonious relationships all around. It is mandatory that we repent of and get rid of false assumptions in our lives if we are to walk like Yeshua!

What is an *assumption*?

1. The act of taking for granted: Assumption of a false theory.
2. Something taken for granted or accepted as true without proof; a supposition: A valid assumption.
3. Presumption; arrogance.

If I were to sum it all up, I would say that a false assumption is *thinking evil* of someone else with no proof. People that judge another because of false assumptions are always sure that they are right. False assumptions + pride + arrogance + judgment go hand in hand. False assumptions happen when we hold grudges against someone in our past, and we begin to judge others according to our experience.

For example, I had a team member that was angry with his mom because he believed that his mom was very possessive when he was growing up. He could not get married for many years, and he was furious. He demanded that I found him a wife and was very forceful about it. Later on I found out that he thought that I will not ever release him to get married because he was angry with his mom for being possessive. He *assumed* that I would also be possessive (as I am an Archbishop, a Pastor, and a mother figure). His relationship with me was based on *false assumptions*. He judged me as *if* I am his mother and of course that caused a wedge in the relationship. His only hope was to truly repent and forgive his mother, and then humble his heart to form a relationship with me and with all other women with no *false assumptions*.

His grudge against his mother had been ruling his life and destroying all his relationships!

Another example from my marriage is when Rabbi Baruch and I got married. It was tough to get through to him. I would talk and he would not listen and would resist me all the way. Finally we concluded that he had a grudge against his mom that rejected him when he was born and spent all of her life "griping" and criticizing him. He *assumed* that every time I talked it was out of rejection and criticism and he *automatically* would be deaf to what I said, he would listen to absolutely nothing. It was so frustrating! Until finally we realized that what was clogging his ears were *false assumptions* about me because of his hurt and grudge towards his mother. After he forgave his mother he started listening and our relationship improved.

There are many more examples, for instance when a woman marries a man and develops instant hostility against him at the first sign of what she would detect as "abuse." That woman had a man molest her when she was little, and anything that can resemble that (though it may not be) is interpreted as "abuse" and her husband does not stand a chance of intimacy with her because of the *false assumption* based on a grudge that does not permit his wife to trust him.

In other situations, some women in ministry are persecuted under the false assumption that all women with strong character are *Jezebels*. One of my team members suffered that kind of persecution because she was anointed and prophetic, very able and capable, so she was labeled a "Jezebel."

This of course devastated her life and for a while affected her walk until Yah healed her. This is an all too common *false assumption* in the Church that is causing unjust behavior towards many great women. I always tell people to be *very careful* when they use the term Jezebel, as Jezebel was a terrible idolater and a witch and how serious it is to call women of God "Jezebels"! This false assumption is grieving the Holy Spirit. In the Middle Ages there were some women prophets in a French town, and they were all burnt at the stake labeled "witches". False assumptions can be *deadly*.

The Jewish people have been victims of false assumptions. Hitler based his entire Antisemitic theology on that. He built on an ancient grudge to most Christians had and still have; "The Jews killed Christ," and so the Jews are evil, and they are to blame for all the evil in society. I still remember a story that my mother told me. She had just hired a maid from a low-income family in Chile. This young woman came to our home and began to stare at my mom's face and head intently. After staring as if searching for something she could not find she asked the most unusual question: "Where are your horns?"

"My horns?" my astonished mom asked.

"Yes," said the young maid, "we have been taught (in the church) that Jews are demonic so they must have horns like the devil!"

In the book of 1 Corinthians 13:5 it says that "Love thinks no evil" (NKJV). In other translations such as the Amplified Bible it says, "(Love) takes no account of the evil done to it [it pays no attention to a suffered wrong]."

In the Strong's Concordance, the word "thinks" is interpreted as follows: Strong's 3049 *Logizomai:*

1. To take into account, weigh, meditate on

2. To suppose, deem, judge
3. To determine, purpose, decide

In other words: Love does not meditate on anything evil about other people, does not judge others, does not purpose or decide evil about them.

Love does not create an evil mental picture about others, does not nurse a grudge, and does not project from unhealed past traumas and experiences into present and future relationships.

False assumptions are harmful because they are based on evil thinking, and evil thinking is opposite to *love,* and Yah (God) is *love.*

I have experienced persecution from some pastors that have *assumed* that because I teach on the Jewish roots of the faith, I put people "under the Law." They have biases in their heart against anything Jewish because Replacement Theology has done a "good job" in causing hostility towards the Torah and the Jewish people. Also there are some Messianic groups that have fallen into the "spirit of religion" rather than the anointing.

So, because of that anything labeled "Messianic" raises some "flags" with many, many pastors in the Church. That is, of course, an outcome of *deadly false assumptions.* Since there are many more non-Messianic congregations and ministries that have fallen under the spirit of religion also and they are not criticized as much. The false assumptions against all that is Jewish is the legacy of many Church Fathers like Constantine, Augustine, John Chrysostom, and even Martin Luther. They left a legacy of false assumptions towards the Jews and everything Jewish that is bringing death to the Church to this day.

I still remember a congregation in Mexico. I had preached in many places, and there was a tremendous outpouring of the Holy Spirit. People flocked after us from church to church, and many came because the radio advertised the miracles that were happening. Finally on Friday night I was scheduled to preach in another town nearby. Since I was exhausted from a week-long of non-stop preaching and this was Shabbat eve (Friday night) I reclined on the pulpit and said: "Shabbat Shalom!" Then I proceeded to explain about Shabbat, and I told them that I would not work, but rather the Holy Spirit will minister miracles as I "rest" in the pulpit. There was such an outbreak of miracles that night: The following night, many people had come from neighboring towns because they had heard about the miracles.

As we were preparing to enter the hall, the assistant pastor conveyed a message to us from the pastor: "Do not preach about anything Jewish, only on Jesus Christ and nothing else!" As he was saying that to us, the lights went off in the church building; the music died off (there was no electricity) and a spirit of mourning set in as if an unseen hand had stopped all the light from coming into that congregation. What a false assumption! As if "Jesus Christ" is not Jewish, but that is precisely what Replacement Theology has done, it has divorced the Messiah from his own identity as a Jew and from His people and His Torah.

Beloved, false assumptions are harmful and even deathly. We have all fallen into them at one time or another; some have even done it in the name of the "Holy Spirit" or "prophetic discernment." This is the opposite of *love* who thinks no evil and believes all things. Love bears up under anything and everything that comes, is ever ready to believe the best of every person, its hopes are fadeless under all circumstances, and it endures everything [without weakening]. (See 1 Corinthians 13:7 AMP.)

May we be ready to believe the *best* (not the worst) of every person in the days to come and nurture loving relationships all around us.

"Love never fails."

— 1 Corinthians 13:8

CHAPTER 17

DISPELLING SUPERSTITIONS AND MYTHS

A lying tongue hates those who are crushed by it.

— *Proverbs 26:28a*

A MYTH IS A widely held but false belief or idea. The Merriam-Webster dictionary describes the word *myth* as follows:

1. *Noun:* An idea or story that is believed by many people but that is not true.

It is incredible how many people believe all kinds of myths and fables. These beliefs are destructive, and they can dismantle relationships, they are based on *fables* and *legends*, on *false beliefs* and *false ideas*. It may be that all of us at one time or another have believed a false rumor or a false report that later on became a full fabled myth, destroying everything in its path.

MASS MURDER

> **No one takes it from Me, but I lay it down of Myself. I have power to lay it down, and I have power to take it again. This command I have received from My Father.**
>
> — John 10:18

Believing false stories based on narrow-minded interpretations can block people from the path of salvation, and it can even cause mass murder like in the case of Hitler's extermination of Jews. Many Germans, Christians included believed that the Jews were to blame for the bad economy of Europe during the Second World War. They actually thought that the Jews were like a vermin that needed to be exterminated with rat poison. Most Christians at the time in every nation believed the fabled myth "The Jews killed Christ" so there is no forgiveness for them.

This myth was established by a well-known orator and Christian leader during the 4th Century who spread the destructive lie, "*all the Jewish people are guilty for killing Christ and for the sin of deicide (killing God) there is no expiation possible!*" This myth propagated like wildfire and caused the humiliation, persecution, torment, and extermination of millions of Jews.

For those who still believe it: First, the Romans killed the Messiah under Roman orders, the Jews had no jurisdiction to execute the death penalty. Second, we all led Him to death since He went to the Cross to pay for all our sins, both Jews and Gentiles. Third, no one killed Him as He said that no one could kill Him and He laid down His life for us. (John 10:18)

HORNS AND A TAIL

I still remember a story my Mom told me when I was a kid. There was a young lady that came from the countryside of Chile to become our maid. When she met my Mom (who was about less than five feet tall, 1.45 meters), she looked all around her on her backside and on top of her head. My Mom was quite puzzled to know what this young maiden was trying to find in her and asked her, "What are you doing?" The girl, in turn, said with wonder, "Where is your tail and where are your horns? The priest in the village told us that all you Jews are children of the devil and that you all have horns and a tail like the devil does." It would be hilarious if it wouldn't be so tragic and destructive!

BLOCK SALVATION

> For I do not desire, brethren, that you should be ignorant of this mystery, lest you should be wise in your own opinion, that blindness in part has happened to Israel until the fullness of the Gentiles has come in.
>
> — Romans 11:25

However, also many Jews have believed fables about Yeshua the Messiah, thus blocking salvation for them. Stories like Him being "a bastard kid that led a revolution," to Him being a friendly Rabbi that "Gentiles made into a god," have stopped up the ears of our people for nearly two millennia! The good news is that no Christians were exterminated because of these fables, but for sure many Jews have been blinded due to these lies from seeing the truth about Yeshua born supernaturally of *Miriam* from the House of David who was a Virgin at the time of His birth fulfilling Isaiah's prophecy:

> Therefore YHVH Himself will give you a sign: Behold, the virgin shall conceive and bear a Son, and shall call His name Immanuel.
> — Isaiah 7:14

Thus they have not been able to *see* Yeshua the Messiah but rather a distorted image of Him as a historical figure.

HATEFUL LIES

> Do not keep silent, O God! For behold, Your enemies make a tumult; And those who hate You have lifted up their head.
> — Psalm 83:1-2

Today there are many myths and fables concocted by the Palestinian Authorities equating Israel to Nazi Germany and Israelis to Nazis. Millions of people all over the world believe those lies that are as removed from reality as the east is from the west. The purpose of these lies is the annihilation of Israel.

> They have said, "Come, and let us cut them off from being a nation, that the name of Israel may be remembered no more."
> — Psalm 83: 4

THE TRUTH

> But I say to you, love your enemies, bless those who curse you, do good to those who hate you, and pray for those who spitefully use you and persecute you.
>
> — Matthew 5:44

Israel is most probably the only country in the world that takes care of her wounded enemies. Israel has assisted wounded Palestinians, Syrians, and Lebanese; and treats in her hospitals many of our hostile neighbors.

The Arabs inside of Israel are the most prosperous in all of the Middle East; they live in the most favorable conditions than anywhere else in any Arab country that you could mention. In Judea and Samaria as it was in *Gush Katif* in Gaza, the Israelis that have settled in our Biblical Land give jobs to potential enemies and they can feed their families. Everywhere else in the Middle East most people are poor with a high rate of unemployment. The only reason why no more jobs are given is that it has become perilous to hire Muslim/Arab ("Palestinian") workers, as too many terror attacks have come from those living among us.

How do myths and fables develop? Hitler said it and did it. These are his infamous words: "Tell a *big lie* enough times, and *everyone* will believe it."

Lies about others are infringing on the Commandment:

You shall not bear false witness against your neighbor!
> — Deuteronomy 5:20

LIES ABOUT OTHERS THAT BECOME MYTHS AND FABLES ARE DESTRUCTIVE

A CONTROVERSIAL HAT

These last few weeks since I have been elevated to the position of Archbishop by the Trans Atlantic and Pacific Alliance of Churches, I have "enjoyed" the written remarks of some judgmental people. One of them stands out especially. It is those that have judged me for wearing the Archbishop's miter in the ceremony of Inauguration in Jerusalem. The said remarks mentioned that I "have submitted myself to "the fish god, Dagon since this hat represents Dagon, so I am under that demonic and pagan principality by wearing this hat and this attire."

> My brethren, let not many of you become teachers, knowing that we shall receive a stricter judgment.
>
> — Ya'akov (James) 3:1

I have no doubts that *many* believe this. But you see: It is not based on truth but rather *interpretations*. There is *no proof* that the miter was patterned after the fish deity-Dagon though it can resemble the fish head from ancient paintings. Also, some of the crowns of ancient kings looked like the miter.

Maybe it is, and maybe it isn't.

When there is no *substantial proof,* all is a matter of *interpretation*. There is no palpable evidence that Dagon is the source of the design of the hat. There are no historical writings that connect the pagan Dagon with the design of the Bishops hat. It would be the same if we interpreted that every woman that wears a head-cover is a Muslim and they have submitted themselves to Islam and Sharia Law. Of course that would be an *interpretation* and an *assumption* based on the fact that head covers look similar when worn by Christian, Hindu, Jewish or Muslim Women, especially the more modern ones.

BEWARE OF EMPHASIS ON EXTERNALS

> Do you look at things according to the outward appearance? If anyone is convinced in himself that he is Messiah's, let him again consider this in himself, that just as he is Messiah's, even so we are Messiah's.
>
> — 2 Corinthians 10:7

It would be the same if we judged Queen Esther for wearing a pagan Persian costume to meet with the pagan King. We could say that she was under deception and that she submitted herself to their pagan treatment. I am sure that she wore a Persian crown when she became Queen. However history amply proves that *she was on a mission*. And she fulfilled her mission as the whole nation of Israel was saved because of her *obedience*.

You can rest assured that by wearing a Bishop's miter I have not submitted myself to any Dagon or fish-god principality: But narrow-minded, self-righteous, and immature believers tend to miss what YHVH is doing by putting too much emphasis on externals.

TONGUES OF FIRE

> Then there appeared to them divided tongues, as of fire, and one sat upon each of them.
>
> — Acts 2:3

The truth is that the two tongues of Bishop's miter represent the Old (*Tanakh*) and the New Testaments that Bishops are to teach from. To the Bishops I know it represents the *Tongues of Holy Fire* that rested on the heads of the Jewish Believers in Messiah when the Holy Spirit fell on them in Shavuot (Pentecost). There are many Bishops and Archbishops of different Christian Denominations that wear this hat without being baptized in the Holy Spirit, as it has become a tradition. In my case it is not a tradition—though the attire is traditional—but rather a reality: I have been fully immersed, visited, and filled with the precious Holy Spirit, Ruach HaKodesh, and He is the source of my strength, anointing and authority.

Some others could say that Bishops dressed in this traditional attire have killed Jews in past years. I am fully aware of that being a Jew myself, but the attire had nothing to do with this, neither did the miter. *In fact people in soldier's uniforms, doctor's gowns, police uniforms, and even no uniform murdered many Jews. Then we should judge and excommunicate anyone wearing these garments, shouldn't we?*

> **Judge not, that you be not judged. For with what judgment you judge, you will be judged; and with the measure you use, it will be**

measured back to you. And why do you look at the speck in your brother's eye, but do not consider the plank in your own eye?

— Matthew 7:1-3

THE STAR OF DAVID

Many people have judged the *Magen David* or *Star of David* as a demonic sign because it is found as "Solomon's Seal" among the Free Masons. Free Masonry is a deceptive, Lucifer worshiping secret brotherhood that in the lowest degrees do "good works" and in its highest degrees worships Lucifer (name of Satan before his rebellion against YHVH). Therefore since the Free Masons use the Star of David, it surely is of demonic origin. There are other assumptions about it, but the point is that we need to be careful not to start a rumor that can be destructive and based on *interpretation*.

THE SIGNATURE OF MESSIAH?

"I, Yeshua, have sent My angel to testify to you these things in the churches. I am the Root and the Offspring of David, the Bright and Morning Star."

— Revelation 22:16

The *Magen David* is made of two superimposed triangles representing the *Shield of David* and possibly the signature of King David, according to Paleo-Hebrew (Ancient Hebrew). It has also been interpreted as the Signature of Messiah Yeshua as one triangle points down (God came down and became flesh) and one points up (He ascended to heaven after His resurrection). Since a triangle is *three-sided,* it could represent

ELOHIM as Triune (Father, Son, and Holy Spirit) and Adam (man) as triune (spirit, soul and body). So all ELOHIM (God) and all Adam (man) is who Messiah Yeshua is.

Ultimately every symbol and design may have been used by former generations that were pagan for one thing or another. These would include the Cross, the Star of David, the Moon and the Stars, different flowers, plants, etc. Primarily Satan is an imitator, and he uses what the Almighty created and perverts it by giving it a twisted meaning. *While we need to be careful not to wear or use something that is undoubtedly proven as a symbol of sin and death like the Swastica for example and other recognized occult and New Age symbols*; we should refrain from taking things out of context and from starting a crusade against someone because of assumptions that may have distorted interpretations.

THE INFAMOUS BDS

> The covenant which He made with Abraham, and His oath to Isaac, and confirmed it to Jacob for a statute, to Israel as an everlasting covenant, saying, "To you I will give the land of Canaan as the allotment of your inheritance.
>
> — Psalm 105: 9-11

The BDS crusade boycotting Israeli products from Judea and Samaria is born out of the fables and the myths that have been believed in the nations about the Land of Israel belonging to the Palestinians and not to the Jews as established in numerous Scriptures. As I said before; believing and acting upon fables can be dangerous, destroy relationships, and even lead to mass murder. We will do well in obeying YHVH's Commandments:

DO NOT BEAR FALSE WITNESS AGAINST YOUR NEIGHBOR!

Before you express judgment over another person, check your sources and research it thoroughly, as there are many myths and fables going around and the tongue can cause a devastating *fire:*

See how great a forest a little fire kindles!
— Ya'akov (James) 3:5b

In any case, we would do well in heeding to the warning words of Yeshua: "Judge not that you may not be judged."

AN IMPORTANT DISCLAIMER

Though we are not to judge by externals, it is very important to make sure that the way we dress gives glory to YHVH. Each one may have our styles, but we need to be very careful not to get dressed with worldly designs that expose our bodies in an unbecoming way (some parts are to be reserved only for our husband or wife: HaleluYah!), and that goes for both men and women.

Many people also use *T-shirts* advertising metal rock bands or other deathly things. Those should be burnt as they glorify the devil! We should not be a banner advertising Satan's agendas. A real change of heart will also manifest in the way we dress: However this is not to say that we all need to be dressed in uniform. Each one of us has different personalities, and the Creator created us differently.

Some well-meaning people insist that women should not wear pants as this is a man's garment. That is not true, for in different cultures men have had skirts (Scotland) and dresses (all over the Middle East), and women have had pants or *sharwals* all over the middle east as well as in India and other places. In our modern society pants are not relegated to men. So we need to be careful not to fall into a religious and dogmatic spirit but *need to dress in modesty with common sense according to the society where we live so no one will malign us unnecessarily. In all things, we are to give glory to Yah and not to cause a stumbling block before others with seductive garments.*

A rule of thumb is to pray and ask The Holy Spirit to help you dress and to ask another more mature believer to assist you with a constructively critical eye.

The same goes concerning cuttings or tattoos. The Word expressly says *not to do it*:

You shall not make any cuttings in your flesh for the dead, nor tattoo any marks on you: I am YHVH.

— Leviticus 19:28

If you have already done it, go ahead and *repent* and never do it again (1 John 1:9). Nowadays it is effortless with a laser to also *remove them*. Let us be marked by ADONAI *only* and not by any tattoos, not even "good ones." Our bodies are *Kadosh* which is "holy, set apart" and they are the Temple of the Holy Spirit.

CHAPTER 18

THE NOAHIDE LIE
ARE THE 7 NOAHIDE LAWS VALID?

> Be diligent to present yourself approved to God as a workman who does not need to be ashamed, accurately handling the word of truth.
>
> — *2 Timothy 2:15*

NOAHIDE LAWS ARE also called "*Noachian Laws*": A Jewish Talmudic designation for seven biblical laws given to Adam and Noah before the revelation to Moses on Mount Sinai and consequently are considered binding upon all humanity.

THE 7 NOAHIDE LAWS (ACCORDING TO CHABAD.ORG)

The 7 Noahide Laws are rules that all of us must keep, regardless of who we are or from where we come.

Without these seven things, it would be impossible for humanity to live together in harmony.

   1. *Do not profane Gd's Oneness in any way.*

Acknowledge that there is a single Gd who cares about what we are doing and desires that we take care of His world.

   2. *Do not curse your Creator.*

No matter how angry you may be, do not take it out verbally against your Creator.

   3. *Do not murder.*

The value of human life cannot be measured. To destroy a single human life is to destroy the entire world—because, for that person, the world has ceased to exist. It follows that by sustaining a single human life, you are sustaining an entire universe.

   4. *Do not eat a limb of a living animal.*

Respect the life of all Gd's creatures. As intelligent beings, we have a duty not to cause undue pain to other creatures.

   5. *Do not steal.*

Whatever benefits you receive in this world, make sure that none of them are at the unfair expense of someone else.

   6. *Harness and channel the human libido.*

Incest, adultery, rape and homosexual relations are forbidden.

The family unit is the foundation of human society. Sexuality is the fountain of life and so nothing is more holy than the sexual act. So, too, when abused, nothing can be more debasing and destructive to the human being.

7. Establish courts of law and ensure justice in our world.

With every small act of justice, we are restoring harmony to our world, synchronizing it with a supernal order. That is why we must keep the laws established by our government for the country's stability and harmony. These laws were communicated by Gd to Adam and Noah, ancestors of all human beings. That is what makes these rules universal, for all times, places and people.

Laws made by humans may change according to circumstance. But laws made by the Creator of all souls over all of time remain the same for all people at all times...

If we would fulfill these laws just because they make sense to us, then we would change them, according to our convenience. We would be our own god. But when we understand that they are the laws of a supreme Gd, we understand that they can not be changed, just as He does not change.

Why are the Noahide Laws especially important today?

Today, we are on the verge of a new era for humankind, a time when we will finally live together in peace and the world will be filled with divine wisdom. Those who keep these basic rules will have a share in that world, since, after all, they took part in making it possible.

Although these teachings were recorded in the sacred Jewish texts, for many centuries Jews were not able to speak about them to the people they lived amongst. But in recent times, the foremost rabbi of the Jewish people in the 20th Century, Rabbi Menachem M. Schneerson, of righteous memory, encouraged Jews to publicize these teachings, so that the world can prepare for the times of peace and wisdom that are swiftly approaching.

Why are they called the Noahide Laws?

These are called the Noahide Laws because they are the heritage of humanity from our oldest ancestors. Since all humanity are descendants of Noah, who survived the Great Flood, all people today are Noahides. (Chabad.org)

IS IT THE TRUTH?

While they seem to be very good moral laws based on Biblical and Rabbinical interpretations, the Noahide Laws is a faulty replacement of the 10 Commandments. They do *not* exist in this particular cluster of laws or with this name anywhere in the Bible.

They are biblical principles interpreted by Talmudic writings. They were made public by a dead Rabbi from

New York that is worshiped by most Hassidic Jews as "King Messiah." Many believe he will rise again and that he is still sending messages today through his writings and some choice disciples that act as mediums to his current 'prophetic messages' from the grave or from "the world to come" - *Haolam Habah* (in Hebrew).

WHY IS IT DECEPTIVE?

> For such men are false emissaries, deceitful workers masquerading as Messiah's emissaries. And no wonder, for even Satan masquerades as an angel of light.
>
> — 2 Corinthians 11:13-14

1. The source of these laws is the Talmud through the writings of a false Messiah from New York who never even visited Israel.
2. It replaces the Foundational Law Code for every society—the 10 Commandments in the Holy Scriptures that were given by YHVH through Moses to the People of Israel to share with the Nations (see Deuteronomy 5; Isaiah 56; Isaiah 42).
3. Subtly it is trying to influence against the Divinity of the Jewish Messiah Yeshua. It does so through the first Noahide law, according to Rabbinical tradition, "God's Oneness," does not allow for the plurality of ELOHIM, the Triune God which is regarded by Rabbinical Judaism as idolatry.
4. It is seeking to unite the world around one World Religion just like Free Masonry, bypassing the need for

the Blood Atonement provided by the Jewish Messiah Yeshua on Golgotha.

The Talmud has become the source of modern-day Rabbinical Judaism rather than the Torah and the Prophets in the Bible. The Talmud comes from the Oral Law or "*Torah she beal Peh.*"

According to Jewish tradition, the Oral "Torah" was passed down orally in an unbroken chain from generation to generation until its contents were finally committed to writing following the destruction of the Second Temple in 70 A.D.

Writing Oral Torah occurred once the Jewish civilization was faced with an existential threat after the primary religious establishment rejected Yeshua from Nazareth as the Promised Messiah and as the ultimate sacrifice for sin.

The Talmud is a mixture of Truth from the Holy Scriptures, fables, religious traditions and lying interpretations of the Bible and even of history – especially as it pertains to the person and life of Yeshua. It discredits His Divinity and Messiah-ship. It is a Replacement Torah and Replacement Messiah Yeshua theology. It is keeping millions of Jews from recognizing the true Jewish Messiah.

WHO ARE THE NOAHIDES?

Nowadays this term is primarily used to refer specifically to those non-Jews who observe the Seven Laws of Noah. According to a Noahide source in 2018, there are over 20,000 Noahides, and the country with the highest number is the Philippines. However, these laws are embraced by others and even government figures that are not labeled Noahides.

THE ANTIDOTE

"Behold, days are coming" —it is a declaration of ADONAI — "when I will make a new covenant with the house of Israel and with the house of Judah— not like the covenant I made with their fathers in the day I took them by the hand to bring them out of the land of Egypt. For they broke My covenant, though I was a husband to them." it is a declaration of ADONAI. "But this is the covenant I will make with the house of Israel after those days" —it is a declaration of ADONAI — "I will put My Torah within them. Yes, I will write it on their heart. I will be their God and they will be My people.

— Jeremiah 31:30-32

Behold My servant, whom I uphold. My Chosen One, in whom My soul delights. I have put My Ruach on Him, He will bring justice to the nations. He will not be disheartened or crushed until He establishes justice on earth. The islands will wait for His Torah.

— Isaiah 42:1, 4

It is time to bring both the written and the Living Torah, Yeshua the Jewish Messiah, to the Nations. This repentance will bring about Sheep Nations that YHVH will call "My people."

Join the United Nations for Israel to start turning *your* nation into a Sheep Nation, one person at a time. Transforming nations will happen through Torah Truth and Ruach Spirit, by embracing the Gospel made in Zion as preached by the Jewish Apostles 2,000 years ago, and by standing for Israel's restoration to her Promised Land and her Living God.

JOIN THE MOST CRITICAL MOVE OF THE SPIRIT IN THE 21ST CENTURY!

> 'In that day many nations will join themselves to A<small>DONAI</small> and they will be My people and I will dwell among you.' Then you will know that A<small>DONAI</small>-Tzva'ot has sent me to you. A<small>DONAI</small> will inherit Judah as His portion in the holy land and will once again choose Jerusalem. Be silent before A<small>DONAI</small>, all flesh, for He has aroused Himself from His holy dwelling."
>
> — Zechariah 2:15-17 (11-13 in other versions)

PART C
TEACHINGS

CHAPTER 19

GROOMING YOUR SPIRIT

THE EFFECTS OF PASSIVITY, NEGLIGENCE, AND PROCRASTINATION

> Cursed be the one who does YHVH's work negligently,
> and cursed be the one who restrains his sword from blood.
>
> *— Jeremiah 48:10*

---

*V*ERY OFTEN, PEOPLE complain about their condition and situation in life. They even blame the devil for all adverse conditions; thus, they remain in vicious circles of defeat, poverty, sickness, frustration, and hopelessness. But it does not have to be that way—I have good news for you today.

It is possible to change the course of your life, finances, marriage, ministry, health, and so on by getting rid of the biggest thieves of blessing: *Passivity, negligence, and procrastination.*

Though these are three distinctive traits, attitudes, and behaviors, they are all interrelated, and they show up together in an unholy tri-unity. The Holy Scriptures are very clear about their fruit, it is the fruit of the curse, and it is terrible.

PASSIVITY: THE ACCEPTANCE OF WHAT HAPPENS, WITHOUT ACTIVE RESPONSE OR RESISTANCE

Passive people usually are victims of abuse. Unfortunately, after they become believers, they still carry "the victim mentality," and they blame external circumstances for their lack of victory, ill health, poverty or bad relationships. They become prey to evil spirits and blame the devil for their troubles instead of arising, fighting and doing what is right! Even if you were abused in the past (many of us were) or you are being abused in the present, you have to renounce being a victim and kick passivity out of your life as it is stealing your destiny. Declare war on passivity (inaction), expose and get rid of the abuse in Yeshua's name!

Many wives, even among believers in Messiah, who are battered and abused, fail to confront their husbands because of extremely erroneous teaching about wives submitting to their husbands. These demonic teachings have destroyed many people's faith and many potentially good marriages. Wives are not to submit to abuse from their husbands, they are not to submit at all costs! Sin must be exposed to the light for it to be treated and eradicated. Satan works in the dark. Stop being a victim of abuse now. Passivity has killed many women before you and people have blamed God! It is time to realize that these teachings of submission are imbalanced and demonic. I urge you to get the book that my husband, Rabbi Baruch Bierman authored, *The Woman Factor* – www.kad-esh.org "Press on Shop." It will change your life and the life of others through you.

PASSIVITY INCURS YAH'S JUDGMENT!

It is selfish, rooted in fear, self-centered, and fueled by self-pity:

> Deliver those who are being taken away to death, And those who are staggering to slaughter, Oh hold them back. If you say, "See, we did not know this," Does He not consider it who weighs the hearts? And does He not know it who keeps your soul? And will He not render to man according to his work?
>
> — Proverbs 24:11-12

> When I say to the wicked, 'You will surely die,' and you do not warn him or speak out to warn the wicked from his wicked way that he may live, that wicked man shall die in his iniquity, but his blood I will require at your hand.
>
> — Ezekiel 3:18

> And I was afraid, and went away and hid your talent in the ground. See, you have what is yours.' But his master answered and said to him, 'You wicked, lazy slave, you knew that I reap where I did not sow and gather where I scattered no seed. Then you ought to have put my money in the bank, and on my arrival, I would have received my money back with interest. Therefore take away the talent from him, and give it to the one who has the ten talents.'
>
> — Matthew 25:25-28

PASSIVE PEOPLE END UP LOSING EVERYTHING

If you have a tendency to lose things or you are stolen from often; if you feel others are unfair to you and you think you are the victim of your circumstances and your upbringing; if you have been abused by your husband, your father, your mother or your school teacher and you are doing nothing about it besides "pity parties" or hiding, then it is the time to repent from passivity and kick the victim mentality out of your life. YHVH will help you out of all the vicious cycles if you put *Him* and *His* ways *first*. His ways do not condone passivity in the face of abuse. Arise and *fight*!

NEGLIGENCE: THE FAILURE TO TAKE PROPER CARE IN DOING SOMETHING

Some accidents are due to negligence – the failure to use reasonable care, resulting in damage or injury to another.

Negligence is a twin brother to carelessness. It is the fertile soil on which poverty takes root. Negligent people make the most dangerous workers as they can bring your business or ministry down! They tend to forget things, and they do things halfway. It is so severe that the Word says that negligent people are *cursed*:

> **Cursed be the one who does YHVH's work negligently, and cursed be the one who restrains his sword from blood.**
> **— Jeremiah 48:10**

Whatever we do for Him needs to be with *all* our heart, with the utmost care, always walking the extra mile. We must be faithful to *fight* in the Spirit through warfare prayer, and with our natural abilities, without holding back *anything*. *Do not restrain your sword from blood* means do not fail to fight the good fight of faith, proclaiming the Word (the Sword of the Spirit), and breaking through all the enemy lines to possess territory for the Kingdom of heaven.

Come out of the curse of negligence today as you *repent* and *make restitution*! If, because of your negligence or carelessness, you have caused damage to others, go and make restitution. If you need to pay, then pay them for what you ruined or ask them what kind of restitution they want. Ask Yah's forgiveness and their forgiveness, and actively bless them and fight for their success. Daniel, in Babylon, was so careful in his work that he was positioned at the right hand of the King, and so was Joseph in Egypt. They were of an *excellent spirit*, which is the opposite of negligence, and earned the highest positions in government.

Arise, repent, make restitution and kick negligence, which is rooted in selfishness and laziness, out of your life: Come out from under that curse and become of an excellent spirit in Yeshua's name! Always do more than required, not less, and anticipate the needs of those you are serving.

> **Now, Israel, what does YHVH your Elohim require from you, but to fear YHVH your Elohim, to walk in all His ways and love Him, and to serve YHVH your Elohim with all your heart and with all your soul,**
>
> **— Deuteronomy 10:12**

NEGLIGENCE BRINGS POVERTY AND DAMAGE

> Poor is he who works with a negligent hand, But the hand of the diligent makes rich.
>
> — Proverbs 10:4

> Beware of being negligent in carrying out this matter; why should damage increase to the detriment of the kings?"
>
> — Ezra 4:22

> He also who is slack in his work Is brother to him who destroys.
>
> — Proverbs 18:9

Get rid of negligence. Become *rich* and a *great blessing* to others by your *diligence*!

PROCRASTINATION: THE ACTION OF DELAYING OR POSTPONING SOMETHING

You cannot trust people that procrastinate. They always have excuses for why things are not done *real-time.* They usually are complainers and extremely self-centered. Everything is always too much for them, so their solution is to do it *later*, but *later* typically never comes!

I always say this: If you have something urgent that needs to be done, give it to a *busy* person. Busy people still find time to do more things, while those that are not busy usually are procrastinators, and you do not want those on your team. You will end up missing the Rapture! The *mañana* spirit means "tomorrow," and it always causes people to stay stuck in their ways with no real success or Kingdom advancing. Procrastination is laziness + passivity + negligence all wrapped up in one.

The antidote for procrastination is *planning*. If you have much to do, then plan when you will do each thing, and ask Abba's help in your planning. Pushing things under the rug will not make them go away. Write yourself a *to-do list* daily. Write it in the order of importance from the most to the least urgent, then go through your list with discipline. At the end of the day pat yourself in the back and praise YHVH for all that you accomplished. Do not sleep on the laurels! Have a good night's rest and keep going tomorrow and the day after and so on, until the end of your days. Busy people can genuinely enjoy their Shabbat *rest*.

> How long will you lie down, O sluggard? When will you arise from your sleep?" A little sleep, a little slumber, a little folding of the hands to rest"— Your poverty will come in like a vagabond and your need like an armed man.
>
> — Proverbs 6:9-11

Procrastinators, just like those who are passive and negligent, become poor. In the case of the procrastinators, poverty overtakes them like an *armed robber*.

Get rid of these *big thieves* and poverty, defeat, destruction, and even ill health will all go out the window. Then you will become a blessing to many, and you will live in *abundance of life*! This blessing is our inheritance in Yeshua.

Beloved, I pray that in all respects you may prosper and be in good health, just as your soul prospers.

— 3 John 2

CHAPTER 20

REMOVING THE LEAVEN OF UNBELIEF
PREPARATION FOR PASSOVER

For seven days no leaven shall be seen with you in all your territory, and none of the flesh which you sacrifice on the evening of the first day shall remain overnight until morning.

— *Deuteronomy 16:4*

THE OTHER DAY I was speaking with my Orthodox sister about the Pesach preparations. The Orthodox Jews take these preparations very seriously. It is an exhausting time of cleaning and removing all traces of "leaven." In the natural, leaven is what causes the flour to rise, and it is a "live organism" as opposed to "leavening agents" such as baking powder that are chemical and dead leaven can keep on multiplying with no limitations. In the New Covenant, "leaven" is both likened unto *sin,* and also as a neutral agent that causes growth and expansion of the Kingdom: So it depends what leaven does. Just like money is neutral, and if used for Kingdom purposes, it is good!

THE NEGATIVE CONNOTATION OF LEAVEN:

> They are all adulterers, like an oven heated by the baker Who ceases to stir up the fire from the kneading of the dough until it is leavened.
>
> — Hosea 7:4

> And Yeshua said to them, "Watch out and beware of the leaven of the Pharisees and Sadducees.
>
> — Matthew 16:6

THE POSITIVE CONNOTATION OF LEAVEN:

> He spoke another parable to them, "The kingdom of heaven is like leaven, which a woman took and hid in three pecks of flour until it was all leavened.
>
> — Matthew 13:33

THE SIN OF DELAYED OBEDIENCE

> They baked the dough which they had brought out of Egypt into cakes of unleavened bread, for it had not become leavened, since they were driven out of Egypt and could not delay, nor had they prepared any provisions for themselves.
>
> — Exodus 12:39

In the story of Passover, "leaven" represents the sin of "delayed obedience." The children of Israel did not have time to wait for the dough to rise or leaven in order to bake their bread for the journey. They had to obey promptly and escape Egypt swiftly.

Thus eating *matza* (unleavened bread) in Pesach is to remind us of their swift obedience. Delayed obedience would have caused the dough to rise, and the people of Israel would have been still slaves in Egypt to this day. Delayed obedience stems from *unbelief*. When we do not believe in His revealed Word and promises, we stall. Stalling cost the wife of Lot her life since she looked back!

Every time we delay obedience, we are going to look back; there will be a yearning for the familiar verses that which is awaiting us as we move forward. That, of course, will bring slavery and death! YHVH is calling us to prompt obedience, unleavened faith.

Especially when it comes to the End-time message of *Teshuva*—the Hebrew word for "repent"—from all sin including Replacement Theology and the pagan religious system, many people tend to stall. They start to look back to their Christmas Trees, Christmas memories, Easter celebrations, pork "delicacies," the acceptance of their home church and other Christians and before you know it their "dough" is leavened, and they cannot move forward and actually die spiritually and sometimes physically because they did not promptly obey the MAP revolution message of repentance. This message is a Prophetic Word to the whole Body of Yeshua and receiving it is a matter of life and death! YHVH is cleansing and repossessing His Bride from

Replacement Theology and all Babylonian system with the lust of the flesh, lust of the eye and pride of life.

NO CONDEMNATION TO WHOM?

> **Therefore there is now no condemnation for those who are in Messiah Yeshua. For the law of the Spirit of life in Messiah Yeshua has set you free from the law of sin and of death.**
>
> **– Romans 8:2**

Many people say, "do not put me under 'condemnation.'" Beloved, there is *no* condemnation to those that walk in the Spirit – meaning led by the Holy Spirit that wrote the Torah, by the Finger of ELOHIM. But there is condemnation for those who walk in their carnal mind and understanding. If we are walking in the Spirit, we will all come to *repentance* from all that is a *lie*, and Replacement Theology is a *lie*!

> **For the mind set on the flesh is death, but the mind set on the Spirit is life and peace, because the mind set on the flesh is hostile toward God; for it does not subject itself to the law of God, for it is not even able to do so, and those who are in the flesh cannot please God.**
>
> **– Romans 8:6-7**

The Holy Spirit is our helper. He helps us to obey YHVH promptly with no delays. When we are in the flesh, we break His Commandments. We are not saved by obedience: Obedience is an outcome of *faith*. True faith will be followed by prompt obedience. That is why the highest form of leaven (sin) is *unbelief*. Unbelief in YHVH, His Word, His power, His character and His promises is belief in something else. We do not live in a vacuum. If we do not trust Him, who or what do we trust?

We are not talking about a "legalistic walk" here but a Holy Spirit, faith empowered walk that seeks to obey Yah promptly whether it is in keeping His Shabbat Holy, His Dietary Laws, giving of tithes and offerings, praying for Israel, ministering healing and deliverance, or keeping yourself pure before marriage. All these things Yeshua did as a perfect Jew (not a religious Jew) and He is calling both Jew and Gentile to follow His example:

> The one who says he abides in Him ought himself to walk in the same manner as He walked.
>
> — 1 John 2:6

He trusted the Father, speaking and performing His Word over every circumstance, even when Satan tempted Him to sin in the desert!

THE HEALING POWER OF THE ROOTS (WRITTEN BY A MINISTRY MEMBER)

> Therefore repent and return, so that your sins may be wiped away, in order that times of refreshing may come from the presence of the LORD; and that He may send Yeshua (Jesus), the Messiah (Christ) appointed for you, whom heaven must receive until the period of

restoration of all things about which God spoke by the mouth of His holy prophets from ancient time.

— Acts 3:19-21

Before Archbishop Dr. Dominiquae's writing of her now-classic book *The Healing Power of the Roots*, she had ministered the first *Back to the Roots* seminar ever in Switzerland. There was so much glory poured out and so many miracles, that on her way home to Israel she asked YHVH a question, "What is so important about preaching the Jewish roots to the Church?"

His answer was clear, "It is a matter of life and death. The Church is like a beautiful rose, cut from her garden, put in a vessel with water for two days. But in the Third Day, if she is not replanted back, she will surely die!"

The Third Day is the Third Millennium as one day is like one thousand years to ADONAI:

> But do not let this one fact escape your notice, beloved, that with the LORD one day is like a thousand years, and a thousand years like one day.
>
> — 2 Peter 3:8

Since Archbishop received this word, she has written many more books and by Yah's grace has created an entire video Bible School called GRM, that is now going to all nations in many languages. The time is late, and YHVH is calling the whole Church to promptly leave the Egypt/Babylon of Replacement Theology. Archbishop's resources can help you do it at the speed of light! But many are "stalling" and waiting for some "favorable time." Now is the favorable time, and there will be no other. This Prophetic Word was received by Archbishop Dominiquae Bierman in 1994 and Yah is accelerating everything, there is really no time to waste:

> You will arise and have compassion on Zion; for it is time to be gracious to her, for the appointed time has come.
>
> — Psalm 102:13

Go to www.kad-esh.org and click on "Shop" to order *The Healing Power of the Roots* now.

LABORERS ARE NEEDED

> For you have not received a spirit of slavery leading to fear again, but you have received a spirit of adoption as sons by which we cry out, "Abba! Father!"
>
> — Romans 8:15

Removing the leaven of unbelief is mandatory as we prepare for Pesach this year. The sin of unbelief affects our walk with Yah. Yeshua said 2,000 years ago that the harvest was plentiful, but the laborers are few. Why there are few is because of *unbelief* which includes *fear*. Some of the most common worries are; fear of the unknown, fear of men, fear of suffering and fear of making mistakes. But fear and unbelief make horrible drivers, and they kill us! Walking in fear is opposite than walking in *love*.

> And He was saying to them, "The harvest is plentiful, but the laborers are few; therefore beseech the LORD of the harvest to send out laborers into His harvest.
>
> — Luke 10:2

YHVH is calling many to lay down their lives for Kingdom purposes, and to answer we have to get rid of the leaven of fear and unbelief.

> **For whoever wishes to save his life will lose it; but whoever loses his life for My sake will find it.**
>
> **— Matthew 16:25**

LEAVEN MANIFESTS ON OUR THOUGHTS AND SPEECH

> **Truly I say to you, whoever says to this mountain, 'Be taken up and cast into the sea,' and does not doubt in his heart, but believes that what he says is going to happen, it will be granted him.**
>
> **— Mark 11:23**

The natural mind is in enmity with ELOHIM. We must have the mind of Messiah and relate to the promises of YHVH as a "done deal." Begin to call things that are not as if they were and stop referring to the circumstances of life as to ultimate reality. King David who was not born again understood this principle. He acknowledged the hardship but always ended in a note of hope and faith. He trusted His Covenant with YHVH beyond his own mistakes and weaknesses and beyond his circumstances. He commanded his soul, mind, will, and emotions to bless YHVH:

> **Bless YHVH o my soul, and all that is within me, bless His holy name. Bless YHVH, O my soul, and forget none of His benefits.**
>
> **— Psalm 103:1-2**

Truly without faith, we cannot please the Almighty. Even if you try your best to obey by your own strength, if you do not put your trust in His strength and promises, you are "leavened" and will be in enmity with ELOHIM:

> And without faith it is impossible to please Him, for he who comes to God must believe that He is and that He is a rewarder of those who seek Him.
>
> — Hebrews 11:6

It is important to declare His Word and promises constantly with your lips. Until you do that, you will not be able to activate the *life* in them. You will have whatever you *say*:

> Death and life are in the power of the tongue, and those who love it will eat its fruit.
>
> — Proverbs 18:21

He can do much more than what we think or ask, but we must *think,* and we must *ask.* It is important to meditate on His Torah-Word and promises if we are to see miraculous outcomes come to pass:

> Now to Him who is able to do far more abundantly beyond all that we ask or think, according to the power that works within us.
>
> — Ephesians 3:20

CIRCUMSTANCES OR PROMISES?

> Watch over your heart with all diligence, for from it flow the springs of life. Put away from you a deceitful mouth and put devious speech

far from you. Let your eyes look directly ahead and let your gaze be fixed straight in front of you.

— Proverbs 4:23-25

Any time that we speak our interpretation of our circumstances rather than Yah's Covenant Word of promise, it is a devious and deceitful mouth and speech!

I am amazed at how many faithful servants of Yah speak unbelief and doubt as a norm—LORD have mercy and forgive us! Many continue speaking circumstances over promises thinking that they are "honest." Well they are "honestly wrong" for if we talk circumstances as the ultimate reality we are calling YHVH a liar, and that is what the snake called Him in the Garden of Eden. All of psychology is based on "speaking what is in your heart to someone else." The snake spoke what was in its heart and led the woman to sin. Unbelief is the original *sin*. Unbelief is where we missed it:

The serpent said to the woman, "You surely will not die! For God knows that in the day you eat from it your eyes will be opened, and you will be like God, knowing good and evil.

— Genesis 3:4-5

How do you *interpret* your adverse circumstances? Are you looking at them through the Word of Yah (God) or your understanding? The woman believed the snake's interpretation of ELOHIM's command and fell into sin. Any time we believe the humanistic, demonic interpretations of our life's circumstances we will fall into the sin of doubting ELOHIM's love and faithfulness.

> You are of your father the devil, and you want to do the desires of your father. He was a murderer from the beginning, and does not stand in the truth because there is no truth in him. Whenever he speaks a lie, he speaks from his own nature, for he is a liar and the father of lies.
>
> — John 8:44

This entire humanistic system, with its "psychological interpretations," is based on unbelief and lies.

King David acknowledged His hardship to YHVH and then went ahead to extol Him and praise Him. *He did not deny he was going through a rough time, but he put his emphasis on ELOHIM's Covenant Promises and abilities and not in his adverse circumstances:*

> O YHVH, how my adversaries have increased! Many are rising up against me. Many are saying of my soul, "There is no deliverance for him in God." Selah. But You, O YHVH, are a shield about me, My glory, and the One who lifts my head.
>
> — Psalm 3:1-2

WHAT ARE YOU SPEAKING?

If I had spoken circumstances instead of promises, I would have had a "vegetable" for a daughter, a dead son, a failure of a ministry, no money so no traveling and no printing of books or creating of Bible School. I would have been handicapped for life after so many falls. My husband would have been sitting in a wheelchair after a terrible accident with broken discs or dead after two heart attacks. I would long ago not be in Eilat because of the persecution and slander suffered from the hands of "believers" and I would have forfeited my call all together as a woman in leadership as it is too hard and unacceptable in many religious circles. I have much more to say about this, but enough is to say this: Because I trusted, declared, and obeyed His Word and promises over all my adverse circumstances, I am still in the ministry and thriving. We are in Eilat and have purchased the Prayer Tower and are about to buy the penthouse next-door to complete the purchase of all the roof apartments. My daughter is tremendously successful in her studies and will soon start her Master's in Education; her friends call her "the Minister of Education" because she is so brilliant and inspired by ELOHIM in all she does. My son is alive, my husband is healthy with a strong heart, and I am up and running to many nations. Goodness and mercy run after me all the time and much, much more!

But I declared all of these much *before* they manifested. When things went wrong, I said – "*all is well with my soul!*" I said it by faith, and then it manifested since you and I can have whatever we *say*:

> You will also decree a thing, and it will be established for you; and light will shine on your ways.
>
> – Job 22:28

We all have "circumstances," and some of us have more adversity than others, but the difference is in whether we have the "leaven of unbelief" or the preciousness of *faith*. What are you thinking and talking?

Moses said to the people, "Remember this day in which you went out from Egypt, from the house of slavery; for by a powerful hand YHVH brought you out from this place. And nothing leavened shall be eaten (thought or spoken).

— Exodus 13:3

CHAPTER 21

RELIGION VS. REALITY
WHAT IS RELIGIOUS DNA… REALLY?

> Then they said, "Come! Let's build ourselves a city, with a tower whose top reaches into heaven. So let's make a name for ourselves, or else we will be scattered over the face of the whole land."
>
> — *Genesis 11:4*

---

*I*F WE WOULD survey many people, young and old and I would pose the question: "What is the 'good old religion,'?" I would probably get some interesting answers. The Baptists would claim it to be the beginning of the Baptist Movement. The Methodists would take us back to John Wesley. The Lutherans would take us back to the 16th Century and Luther's Reformation. The Pentecostals would want us to return to the Azusa Street Revival in L.A., and the Catholics maybe to the times of the Spanish Inquisition or the Crusades from Europe to establish "the kingdom" in Jerusalem. Whichever way we look at it, there would not be a clear consensus among all the denominations of Christianity about "the good old religion." Where are we supposed to "go back to" and which "revival" are we waiting for?

However, they would all agree on one thing: Christianity, as we know it, was established in year 325 through the Council of Nicaea by the "venerated" Byzantine Emperor Constantine of Eastern Rome (Turkey of today). He is venerated because finally during his days there was peace for the Christians who complied with him becoming the First Pope (after Peter) and with a complete divorce from the Jews and everything Jewish. He wrote the following in the Council of Nicaea that established Christianity as we know it.

THE COUNCIL OF NICAEA

The following excerpt is from the letter of the Emperor (Constantine) to all those not present at the council (found in Eusebius, Vita Const. Lib III 18-20).

We ought not therefore to have anything in common with the Jew, for the Savior has shown us another way: our worship following a more legitimate and more convenient course (the order of the days of the week). And consequently, in unanimously adopting this mode, we desire, dearest brethren, to separate ourselves from the detestable company of the Jew.

But even if this were not so, it would still be your duty not to tarnish your soul by communication with such wicked people (the Jews). You should consider not only that the number of churches in these provinces make a majority, but also that it is right to demand what our reason approves, and that we should have nothing in common with the Jews. (Fordham.edu)

Constantine is venerated because he brought the Church the established celebrations of Sun-Day worship, Easter (*Ishtar*) worship, Christmas (Saturnalia) worship, All Saints/Halloween worship. He is venerated because he established the Culture of Christianity as we know it today which unleashed terrible persecutions, humiliations, and massacres against the Jews for many generations through Crusades, Inquisitions, pogroms, and the Holocaust.

Therefore, it is no surprise that when looking forward to *unity* that is the key for revival and salvation of all nations, all denominations of Christianity—Protestants, Evangelicals, and Catholics—would rally around the origins of Christianity which is the "good old religion" established by Eastern Roman Emperor Constantine, wholly divorced from its Jewish roots. *He is the common denominator that all major denominations of Christianity would agree upon.* Constantine is the point of *unity*.

Constantine and his Christianity has become the Bridegroom of the Christian Church.

THE FOLLOWING IS FROM CHRISTIANITY TODAY:

Four years ago, in Istanbul, a humble Turkish book partially reversed the 11th Century's Great Schism. Catholics joined Eastern and Oriental Orthodox—alongside Protestants—to publish a slim, 12-chapter treatise on their common theological beliefs.

There was a "wall of enmity" separating Protestants and Orthodox in Turkey, said Behnan Konutgan, former head of the Turkish Evangelical Alliance. As the dialogue progressed, most evangelicals were "suspicious." But about a decade ago, Konutgan and Schirrmacher began regular yearly visits with Orthodox leaders. Reconciliation was a key goal because a Turkish Protestant pastor had slandered Orthodoxy's global head, Ecumenical Patriarch Bartholomew I.

Together they set up a procedure to handle such complaints. Shortly thereafter, Schirrmacher launched extensive religious liberty advocacy by the WEA for the Eastern Christian church.

"Many evangelicals are short-sighted, not realizing the Orthodox and Catholics have been here for hundreds of years," Konutgan said. "If they read this book, they will see we believe in 90 to 95 percent of the same things."

So, whether it is nudging conservative Protestants toward Christian unity or ancient churches toward understanding evangelicals, Schirrmacher believes in the power of engagement. "Evangelicalism is the search for the DNA of Christianity," he said. "But then other churches take it over. Suddenly it is no longer a specific evangelical conviction, but a Christian one." (Casper)

Please bear in mind that Constantine established the Christianity that replaced the original Gospel made in Zion in *Turkey*. This new (and old) unity among all Christian denominations is coming from *Turkey again*. Hmm...

IS "THE GOOD OLD RELIGION" THE TRUE DNA?

So, in search for the DNA of Christianity, they found that the "good old religion" established by Emperor Constantine is the common denominator and that all denominations can agree about 90-95% with each other. The issue is that if we talk DNA in a biological way (which is a type and shadow from the Spiritual DNA), 5% to 10% mutation from the norm could mean severe malformations of the cells, horrendous and incurable diseases and early death.

The following will give us an idea of what DNA Mutations can do and remember: *The same can happen when there are spiritual DNA mutations.*

AN EXCERPT FROM THE U.S. NATIONAL LIBRARY OF MEDICINE:

> To function correctly, each cell depends on thousands of proteins to do their jobs in the right places at the right times. Sometimes, gene mutations prevent one or more of these proteins from working properly. *By changing a gene's instructions for making a protein, a mutation can cause the protein to malfunction or to be missing entirely.*

When a mutation alters a protein that plays a critical role in the body, it can disrupt normal development or cause a medical condition. A condition caused by mutations in one or more genes is called a genetic disorder.

In some cases, gene mutations are so severe that they prevent an embryo from surviving until birth. These changes occur in genes that are essential for development, and often disrupt the development of an embryo in its earliest stages. *Because these mutations have very serious effects, they are incompatible with life.* (Medlineplus.gov)

ARE WE LOOKING TO RESTORE A MUTATED DNA?

The question is the following: What DNA are we looking for? The DNA of the "good old Christianity"? Or are we looking for the DNA of *The Way*. And is *The Way* the same as Christianity?

> **Yeshua said to him, "I am the way, the truth, and the life! No one comes to the Father except through Me.**
>
> **– John 14:6**

Here is another critical question: Did Yeshua (commonly called Jesus) the Jewish Messiah bring forth Christianity or did He bring The Way of the Kingdom of heaven? Did Paul bring forth Christianity or the Gospel (Good News) to the Gentiles?

Are we to *unite* around a religious system established by the manipulations of Scripture of a Sun worshiping Roman Emperor, backed up by lukewarm and compromised Gentile Bishops in Turkey over 300 years after Yeshua handed His

Gospel to His Jewish Disciples; or are we to *unite* around *Truth* as spoken by the Jewish Apostles and Hebrew Prophets of old?

> You have been built on the foundation made up of the (Jewish) emissaries (Apostles) and (Hebrew) prophets, with (Jewish) Messiah Yeshua Himself being the cornerstone.
> — Ephesians 2:20

THE TRUE DNA

> But if some of the branches were broken off and you—being a wild olive—were grafted in among them and became a partaker of the root of the olive tree with its richness, do not boast against the branches. But if you do boast, it is not you who support the root but the root supports you.
> — Romans 11:17-18

When in search of the *true DNA* to the faith community, we will find the DNA to be heavenly and Jewish. We will find a Jewish Messiah without a trace of Roman in His blood, cells or theologies (Matthew 1; John 4:22). We will find a New Covenant made with the House of Israel and the House of Judah (Jeremiah 31:31-34). We will find an Israeli Olive Tree that the Gentiles are grafted into (Romans 11). We will find the Torah, and Yah's Holy Commandments need to be written in our hearts by the Holy Spirit who is God or ELOHIM (Matthew 5:17-21). We will find Davidic Worship with singing, dancing, and creativity celebrating Shabbat and the Holy Feasts as given by YHVH to Israel (See Leviticus 23).

When searching for the true DNA, we will also find the true *Shavuot* (Pentecost) through the baptism of the Holy Spirit and Fire, with speaking in tongues, miracles, casting out demons, prophesying, raising the dead and healing the sick. This baptism empowers us to do the works of the Kingdom with divine ability and passionate intimacy with our Bridegroom, the Lion of Judah, the Jewish Messiah Yeshua (see the Book of Acts) who will soon return to His people Israel and to Jerusalem (See Zechariah 14). *We also will find a Bride, who like Ruth, loves Israel unconditionally and looks to Jerusalem, not to Rome for Spiritual Pilgrimage and allegiance (Book of Ruth).*

Those Christians who *unite* and settle for a mutated Roman DNA coming from *Turkey* with 5% to 10% error, will be experiencing early death, untold spiritual woes and deceptions that will bring about misery, even worse than the one that was experienced in the Dark Ages, which is where that "good old religion" brought us to in the past.

WE INVITE YOU TO UNITE AROUND THE REAL DNA TO THE BRIDE OF MESSIAH.

This pure DNA is the genetic material of a Jewish Messiah, with Jewish roots, with Torah, the Holy Spirit and Fire, the Biblical Feasts, and with an unconditional love for Israel who is the Mother of the Nations.

Ruth replied to Naomi, her Jewish Mother in Law;

> "Do not plead with me to abandon you, to turn back from following you. For where you go, I will go, and where you stay, I will stay. Your people will be my people, and your God my God. Where you die, I will

die, and there I will be buried. May Adonai deal with me, and worse, if anything but death comes between me and you!"
— Ruth 1:16-17

Join the *United Nations for Israel*, also called UNIFY, to fulfill what Yeshua prayed in John 17:

"Make them holy in the truth. Your word is truth... "I pray not on behalf of these (Jewish Disciples) only, but also for those (Gentiles) who believe in Me through their message, that they all may be one. Just as You, Father, are in Me and I am in You, so also may they be one in Us, so the world may believe that You sent Me.
— John 17:17, 20-21

He did not pray for all denominations of Christianity (that did not exist then) to be united, not even all denominations of Judaism. He prayed for Jewish believers and Gentile believers to become *one* like Ruth (Gentile) and Naomi (Jewish) became *one* and brought forth King David and the Messiah, the Son of David. (See the Genealogy of Yeshua in Matthew 1)

I believe that the *United Nations for Israel* is like *Noah's Ark* for our times, and you are invited to come in and be restored to the original DNA, the original Gospel made in Zion, before YHVH shuts the door:

By faith Noah, when warned about events not yet seen, in holy fear prepared an ark for the safety of his household. Through faith he condemned the world and became an heir of the righteousness that comes by faith.
— Hebrews 11:7

CHAPTER 22

IS THERE A CURE FOR RELIGION?

> Now it came about in the course of those many days that the king of Egypt died. And the sons of Israel sighed because of the bondage, and they cried out; and their cry for help because of their bondage rose up to God.
>
> — *Exodus 2:23*

MANY TIMES I have asked myself, *"Why did it take YHVH 430 years until He delivered the people of Israel from Egypt? Why did He let them suffer for so long?"* And I believe that the answer is that they were not desperate enough to be delivered. This determination applies to everything in our life. Whatever our bondage is; only when we are desperate enough, and we are aware of our sickness and need, then we can be delivered.

'On hearing this, Yeshua said, "It is not the healthy who need a doctor, but the sick. But go and learn what this means: {I desire mercy, not sacrifice}. For I have not come to call the righteous, but sinners."'
— Matthew 9:12-13

Yeshua was able to touch, heal, and delivered *all* who came to Him, but the religious folk that was around Him all the time, for the most part, were untouched by Him. They were too full of their own "self-righteousness" to recognize their sickness (religion) and their need (salvation).

The worst sin of man is being religious. Religiosity leads to a spirit of legalism, judgment, and bitterness. Yeshua was very gentle with the sinners, but very harsh with the religious:

"You brood of vipers, how can you, being evil, speak what is good? For the mouth speaks out of that which fills the heart."
— Matthew 12:34

"You blind guides, who strain out a gnat and swallow a camel!"
— Matthew 23:24

"Woe to you, Scribes and Pharisees, hypocrites! For you clean the outside of the cup and of the dish, but inside they are full of robbery and self-indulgence."
— Matthew 23:25

Religion is a terminal disease with no hope left. It is a matter of life and death for us to know what are the symptoms of the "Disease of Religion" so you can treat them before they take your life and the life of others!

- *Hypocrisy* – Pretending to be "good" but having a heart full of anger, bitterness, criticism, judgment, and pride. This mask leads to self-deception and denial (see Matthew 7:5 and Matthew 23: 25-35).
- *Self-righteousness* – This is the most dangerous symptom; a person thinks that he is "right" and is willing to do *anything* to prove it. All crusades and the Spanish Inquisition were directed by this spirit that executed "justice" against the Jews. This symptom can be a murderous spirit (see Luke 18:9-14).
- *Rigidity* – Seeing everything as "black or white" with absolutely no hope for mercy or process. This spirit is not able to develop any relationship with God or with people. It is totally legalistic, and it always puts people under judgment (see John 8:1-11).
- *Ruthless* – A person that is sure of being "right" will always be cruel and merciless with others that are "wrong." This spirit will justify any means to achieve its end, which is to prove "its rightness" in the name of God and His Kingdom. It will violate boundaries, become abusive and will overrule other people's self will. Hitler's regime displayed this spirit very clearly, and Hitler based the Final Solution on Martin Luther's Book *On the Jews and their Lies* where he called to "execute sharp mercy" (in the name of God) towards the Jews. He was offended by them and became very bitter against them.*

---

* See our free download of *The MAP Revolution* at www.kad-esh.org

Most people will not have the extreme conditions, but any signs of these symptoms should be taken very seriously, if untreated they can turn into a full-blown "Disease of Religion." The best treatment for the early signs to symptoms is simply this: An ample dosage of humility together with forgiveness; take every time that the symptoms reoccur.

HUMILITY

> "But He gives a greater grace Therefore it says, "God is opposed to the proud, but gives grace to the humble." Submit therefore to God, resist the devil and he will flee from you. Draw near to God and He will draw near to you Cleanse your hands, you sinners; and purify your hearts, you double-minded. Be miserable and mourn and weep; let your laughter be turned into mourning and your joy to gloom. Humble yourselves in the presence of the LORD, and He will exalt you."
>
> — James 4:6-10

FORGIVENESS

In his very well-known book, *The Bait of Satan* John Bevere says:

> Medical doctors and scientists have linked unforgiveness and bitterness with certain diseases such as arthritis and cancer. Many cases of mental sickness are tied to bitter unforgiveness. A person who cannot forgive has forgotten the great debt for which they were forgiven. When you realize that Jesus (Yeshua) delivered you from eternal death and torment, you will release others unconditionally. (Bevere)

True forgiveness does not demand "justice." As long as you are demanding "justice" or think that you need to "execute justice yourself" you have not forgiven. That is a very hazardous situation. This sign is the serious warning that Yeshua gives us about unforgiveness (which includes lack of releasing, demanding "justice" and the like). In the Greek culture to *forgive* means to "pardon" someone without releasing them or forgetting. In Hebrew culture, forgiveness is an inner force that brings total healing and includes a complete release of debt. As long as we are holding unto a little bit of grudge or demands for justice, it is not true forgiveness, and it will poison the whole individual. The Disease of Religion is fueled by unforgiveness, victim mentality, and self-righteousness.

> "For if you forgive others for their transgressions, Your heavenly Father will also forgive you." But if you do not forgive others, then your Father will not forgive your transgressions."
> — Matthew 6:14-15

Unforgiveness can cost you your salvation. When the Father does not forgive you, then you have to pay for your sins. What opens the door for the disease? I have found these three factors working together:

- Spiritual Pride
- Bitterness
- Jealousy

These are the same factors that induced the snake to tempt the woman to eat of the Tree of Religion, the Tree of

Knowledge of Good and Evil. "You will not surely die," the serpent said to the woman.

> "For Elohim (God) knows that when you eat of it your eyes will be opened, and you will be like Elohim, knowing good and evil."
> — Genesis 3:4-5

Satan through the snake worked on the woman to get some more knowledge (spiritual pride) and convinced her that ELOHIM did not love her enough to give it to her (bitterness). He told her that ELOHIM did not want them to be like Him (jealousy). These three factors are in the character of Satan who tried to lift himself to be like ELOHIM because of pride, bitterness, and envy. Satan is also jealous of all humanity because we got what he *coveted*. We were created in the image and likeness of the Creator, but he was created lower than that as an angel. (See Psalms 8:4-6; Isaiah 14:13-16.)

Jealousy is a tremendously evil force that has caused more crimes than anything, starting from Cain who was jealous of Abel.

> "Wrath is fierce and anger is a flood, but who can stand before jealousy?"
> — Proverbs 27:4

Cain had the Disease of Religion as he gave a "sacrifice" to ELOHIM but not with his whole heart. He had spiritual pride, so when ELOHIM did not accept his half-hearted sacrifice, he got angry, and the true issue came out: He was jealous of his brother Abel. Abel was an honest, humble worshiper and was not trying to show off. Cain was full of pride, bitterness, and jealousy and ended killing Abel. The Disease of Religion is very dangerous:

> "But for Cain and for his offering He had no regard so Cain became very angry and his countenance fell. Cain told Abel his brother. And it came about when they were in the field, that Cain rose up against Abel his brother and killed him."
>
> — Genesis 4:5-8

Throughout Church History, we can see the Disease of Religion raising brothers to kill brothers. After the Council of Nicaea when the spirit of religion possessed the Church, the Christians started killing the Jews. Later on after the reformation also, Christians killed Christians all in the name of God. The whole history of the reformers is riveted with blood and cruel battles between brothers. They were all trying to prove that they were "right," and by doing so they hurt the Father who is the only One that is *right* and *righteous*. They crucified the Son *afresh* by hating and killing each other!

The Disease of Religion has polluted every move of God. Things that start in the Spirit end in the flesh because of spiritual pride, bitterness, and jealousy.

As Yah has entrusted us with the End-time Message of *Restoration* of the Ecclesia to the original Hebrew foundations of faith, I prayed that this time the Disease of Religion would not take over. *No more killing in the name of God, truth, or justice*. It is high time that we follow the way of the Lamb even if He is also a Lion roaring from Zion. He taught us to *forgive* and never to retaliate, to love our enemies, to bless those who curse you, to love those who hate us. He cried from the Cross for all humanity to hear:

> "Father forgive them, they do not know what they do."
> — Luke 23:34

If we follow His example of unconditional *love* and *mercy* we will be immune to the Disease of Religion, and finally, *love* will prevail, and the world will *know* that the Father sent Yeshua (John 17:21).

> "He (Yeshua) began saying to His disciples first of all, 'Beware of the leaven of the Pharisees, which is hypocrisy.'"
> — Luke 12:1b

CHAPTER 23

THE EFFECTS OF RELIGION
ARE YOU A SPIRITUAL ORPHAN?

*For whoever does the will of My Father who is in heaven,
he is My brother and sister and mother."*

— Matthew 12:50

---

*M*ANY PEOPLE NOWADAYS are spiritual orphans as they do not seem to have someone they can call a spiritual parent. This spiritual orphanhood is manifested through a lack of tithing or incorrect tithing. Many have grown disappointed with various teachings and preachings about the subject of giving, and they have entirely "thrown out the baby with the bathwater." *However, tithing to those who teach you is an act of love and honor that removes spiritual orphanhood!* Follow me in this Torah based teaching that will change your life forever.

PRESCRIBED TITHES AND WHO RECEIVES THEM

One of the significant subjects that run through the Holy Scriptures is the subject of prescribed giving. This subject has been very controversial throughout the years within the different denominations. Some have abused the whole matter on Holy Giving, and others have discarded it altogether, saying that it is done away with. Others are tithing, but not correctly, failing to give the tithes to the people for which it was intended.

> To the sons of Levi, behold, I have given all the tithe in Israel for an inheritance, in return for their service which they perform, the service of the tent of meeting.
>
> — Numbers 18:21

YHVH said the tithe is holy, *Kadosh* which means "set apart" from all the rest of your money. This set-apart portion is to be given to the Levites and the *Kohanim* (the Hebrew word for "Priests") who are the ministers and the priests that carry the spiritual authority for the wellbeing of the people. The New Testament is even more explicit, and it merely says to give to those that teach you the Word. (See Galatians 6:6-8.)

I wrote a book called *Restoration of Holy Giving* that I believe can change your spiritual life and your finances.[*]

A MATTER OF THE HEART

Tithing, and giving in general, is not a money issue, it is actually about the *heart*. The condition of our hearts will always manifest in the way we give. Meditate on the following:

---

[*] Go to www.kad-esh.org and press on "Shop" to order.

For where your treasure is, there will your heart be also.
— Matthew 6:21

Whatever you value, whatever you *love*, you will spend your money on. For example, if you treasure family time, you will spend your money on family and family vacations. If you love fashion, you will spend your money on clothing. If you love missions or if you love Israel you will spend your money on those causes and so on. The way you spend your money denotes the condition of your heart.

DO YOU LOVE YOUR MENTORS?

Your tithes need to go to your spiritual mentors, pastors, bishops, or leaders. It is a matter of order. Just like when things are in order in our bodies then our blood flows, when things are in spiritual order, the blessing flows.

If you are a tither, but your tithes are going to missions or the poor, then, although you mean well, things are not in spiritual order. To tithe correctly and have things in spiritual order, you are commanded to give your tithes to your spiritual authorities or to those who mentor you in the faith. You should give to missions and the poor, but these gifts come from offerings, your tithes belong to your spiritual mentors!

If you do not have a pastor, mentor, someone that encourages you, or someone whose teachings you love, then this is a heart issue.

Maybe you have a root of bitterness in your heart against your pastors or spiritual authorities from the past? Perhaps you grew disappointed in them. If so, you would do well to do some heart maintenance and forgive them. This work of forgiveness will allow for the opening of your heart to receive new teachers, new pastors, and new mentors and honor them.

DO YOU FEED ON CYBERSPACE?

Like many, you may not be in a typical church right now. Maybe you have not found a congregation that meets on Shabbat or who loves the Holy Spirit and the Torah; maybe you live in a spiritual desert. You can still start doing the right thing concerning your tithes.

Take the time to think, pray, and ask yourself, "Who is ministering to me spiritually? What preacher/teacher/rabbi is mentoring me through the internet, T.V., books, or through prayer? We are living in a Cyber-world and, therefore, many are being mentored by what ministers and ministries publish on the internet: On T.V.; Radio; Facebook; YouTube; Spreaker or other podcasts; email, etc.

> **Now let the one who is taught the word share all good things with his teacher. Do not be deceived—God is not mocked. For whatever a man sows, that he also shall reap. For the one who sows in the flesh will reap corruption from the flesh. But the one who sows in the Ruach will reap from the Ruach eternal life.**
>
> — **Galatians 6:6-8**

WHO IS YOUR CONGREGATION?

Not long ago, a lady came to our Bible Center when I was not in, and she filled out a welcome card. One of the questions on that card is: "What congregation do you belong to?" I was quite amazed when her answer was "*you*." I had never met this precious lady, so how can she say that we are her congregation?

On top of it, she had never come to any of our monthly meetings, how can this be?

My secretary explained this mystery to me, "She watches you on T.V. in her area, Archbishop!"

Where she lives there is no Messianic Apostolic Prophetic congregation yet, so my teachings on T.V. are feeding her to the point where, in her heart, she belongs to our congregation, though she watches me on T.V.

I wonder how many people are being fed by our teachings via email, T.V., Facebook, Spreaker, LinkedIn and YouTube and consider Kad-Esh MAP Ministries their Cyber congregation! And yet, not all of them are tithing to us. Why is that?

> **I also discovered that the portions of the Levites had not been given them, so that the Levites and the singers who performed the service had gone away, each to his own field.**
> **– Nehemiah 13:10**

When the tithes are not given as prescribed to the ones they belong to, many ministers and leaders find themselves struggling very much financially as they have to pay their bills on top of investing in the ministry. They have many more bills than ordinary people do! Many of them can feel tempted to leave the ministry altogether and take a job. This causes more spiritual orphanhood to be released as ministers are missing in action.

HONOR YOUR MENTORS

There is a significant lack of knowledge about the importance of *honoring* Yah by honoring the ones who teach His Word and mentor you in His Kingdom. When we do not honor our mentors, teachers, and ministers, we become spiritual orphans. The first commandment with a promise is the following:

> 'Honor your father and your mother just as ADONAI your God commanded you, so that your days may be long and it may go well with you in the land ADONAI your God is giving you.
>
> — Deuteronomy 5:16

SPIRITUAL PARENTS CHANGE YOUR LIFE

I am a perfect example of how a spiritual parent can change a life. Because I was called sovereignly like Paul the Apostle, no one can claim to have led me to the Kingdom.* Another issue is that I'm a woman in a leadership position, and when my ministry began in the '90s, not many accepted women in ministry. I had no mother and no father in the spirit. I asked YHVH, "What shall I do? How do you want me to be a Mother of Nations if I have no spiritual mother?" He said to me clearly, *"Choose one!"*

I carefully contemplated all the women in my life, and I chose one. It required me to humble myself to do this! I was a proud orphan as I have had to overcome all the hardships alone. Because of the revolutionary message I carry not many wanted to support us, especially back in the '90s. Sometimes those that were pastoring us even rejected us. Because of this lack of support and rejection, we went through much hardship for many years as we started our ministry. But YHVH spoke to me, "Choose a spiritual mother."

---

* My book *Yes!* has the whole story: www.kad-esh.org. Press on "Shop."

I considered all the women in my life, and these are the questions that helped me choose:

1. Who is a godly woman of faith I can learn from?
2. Who cares for me and wants to see me bloom in the ministry?

I knew Lorie Klein was the answer to my questions. She was thrilled when I chose her as she loved me and supported the vision I had until her last breath on earth; we had a wonderful relationship! She made me promise, as she was passing onto glory on her death bed, that I would never stop playing the guitar. I promised, and therefore you will see that my ministry includes preaching, teaching, writing, and singing with my guitar. Since I made that promise I have recorded four albums with new songs from Yah, many of them are being sung all over the world. *Spiritual parents truly do change your life!*

When we were sent to the USA recently, I had to choose who to send my tithe to here in America. You may be curious about our need to pay tithes, after all, we have been in full-time ministry for many, many years. We have disciples all over the world. I am an Archbishop; why would we be tithing to anyone? We are the ones to receive tithes, are we not?

And yet the Torah teaches us that the Levites always had to give the Tithe of Tithes to the High Priest; therefore, we tithe to our *up-line* in the ministry. Did that minister raise me in the faith? No, he did not. But, he is in the organization where I was ordained as an Archbishop. He is my up-line in America, and he is a wonderful man of Yah who has supported and encouraged our vision and mission in the USA. His blessing means the world to us, just like the blessing of Melchizedek meant to Abraham. (See Genesis 14:19-20.)

> The priest, the son of Aaron, shall be with the Levites when the Levites receive tithes, and the Levites shall bring up the tenth of the tithes to the house of our God, to the chambers of the storehouse.
> — Nehemiah 10:38

THE BLESSING OF YOUR SPIRITUAL PARENTS

Every evening and morning, and every Shabbat we pray and bless all of our natural and spiritual children and disciples worldwide. We believe that our prayers and blessings are making a difference! However, some of these children need to learn to honor with their tithes and their first-fruits offerings so that the fullness of the promise can be fulfilled:

> Honor YHVH with your wealth and with the first of your entire harvest. Then your barns will be filled with plenty, your vats will overflow with new wine.
> — Proverbs 3:9-10

When your mentor, pastor, leader or spiritual *up-line* blesses your First Fruits offerings, the blessing comes to *rest*, to *stays* in your house. It does not come and go! Why is this? Because this is the spiritual principle of the blessing in the Torah. Our *honor-giving* to those that are our spiritual parents, leaders, pastors, and teachers carries the blessing and YHVH cannot deny His Word!

> The first of all the first fruits of everything and every offering of every kind from all your offerings will belong to the Kohanim (Priests or Ministers). You will also give the kohen the first of your dough, to make a blessing to rest on your house.
> — Ezekiel 44:30

Sometimes you have more than one pastor or teacher that ministers to you. In that case, you can pray and see how Yah leads you to distribute the tithes and the first-fruits offerings.

Love and honor your spiritual parents, your teachers, mentors, leaders, those who pastor you and encourage you. Love and honor those that give Yah, and you, their best to light your path in Yeshua, and your life will be transformed. The Word makes it abundantly clear that love and honor are demonstrated through your tithes (the first 10% of what you earn monthly) and first-fruits offerings (the first of everything, for example your first day of work and its pay).

There is no way for you to pay for what they have had to sacrifice, or the path they have had to walk to establish a ministry and bring you the Word, but you must love and honor, and that means: *Tithes and first-fruit offerings*. Then the blessing will rest in your house, and it shall be well with you.

Then you will *rejoice* over those who serve you and mentor you, and they will rejoice in you!

> On that day men were also appointed over the chambers for the stores, the contributions, the first fruits and the tithes, to gather into them from the fields of the cities the portions required by the

law for the priests and Levites; for Judah rejoiced over the priests and Levites who served.

— Nehemiah 12:44

CHAPTER 24

WOUNDED BY RELIGION
THE STORY OF ARCHBISHOP DOMINIQUAE'S ASSISTANT

"For the letter kills, but the Ruach gives life."

— *2 Corinthians 3:6b*

WHAT MADE ME, as a 14-year-old girl, to make a staunch decision to stop being a believer and reject Jesus for good?

I was raised as a daughter of Pentecostal believers; my grandfather was a preacher. His father was a Jew from Poland, who had resettled to Russia and married a lady from Siberia. When my grandfather was five years old, his father died, and a few years later, they escaped through the border to Finland (during World War II). He worked in hard labor in the forest as a young boy. As a result of that and malnourishment, he was very sickly all his life and even developed a hump on his back. He found his comfort in the Pentecostal church, becoming an evangelist and a preacher. He did not know much about the Holy Spirit but made sure that sin was thoroughly defined. He softened in his old days though. I remember how I read the Bible to him when he was already almost wholly blind. I had a full punk make up then, but he could not see it – so he just smiled as I read his favorite Scriptures and sang him his dearest song, *The Beautiful Land*, where he yearned to go. Not long after these days his time to go to that land came, following my grandmother who had passed away before.

Like my grandfather, I wanted to be an evangelist. Through all my childhood, I was passionate for Jesus, evangelizing my school mates and our neighbors. I attended the annual charismatic summer camps with my best friend, who's church I had begun to go to. After my parents allowed me to read *Run Baby Run* by Nicky Cruz at the age of 10, I wanted nothing else than to become a street evangelist in New York City. I received many prophesies of having a calling from God for His work. I could not wait for an exciting future! I could not comprehend why anyone would want to smoke or drink – even a little mistake made me plead God's forgiveness desperately and feel overbearing guilt. I had underlined many judgment passages from my Bible like, "For sin's payment is death," leaving away the ending part about grace. I felt responsible not only for my own salvation but for everyone's around me. The burden was heavy.

Passionate in my faith, but forever guilty – that was the story of my childhood. I sensed the Holy Spirit and the presence of Yeshua and felt tremendous joy – but on the other hand, I always felt guilty and under judgment. Thus, I became a proficient judge of myself and others. I tried to be a savior – I tried to fix everybody. I tried to force people to believe. Because if they would not, I thought it would be all my fault. I loved and hated God. I was desperately yearning for love and acceptance, but there was no one I could really talk to. I tried to control my life, and I hated to be controlled. My parents say that I was the most stubborn kid anyone could imagine – giving up or even just losing in a game made me so terrified that I made sure to argue endlessly. Showing weakness would mean that I failed – failed to be perfect and failed to control myself to gain security. I was lonely, but at the same time I felt powerful – I could survive, manage, make people believe, and correct my parents to become better believers.

I had a strong character, was a born leader, one that came up with new game-plays and directed other kids. I made a whole row of teenagers leave a gospel concert we were attending because I claimed that using drums in worship was sinful. I had become a member of that congregation where my best friend and her family belonged, and in there any other instruments but piano and guitar were strictly prohibited (as well as clapping hands). According to them, this was the only right church to be a part of. In reality it was more like a cult. But at the same time and because people were so hungry, the Holy Spirit touched us in the summer camps, and we prayed sometimes for hours in tongues. That revival flame was soon roughly extinguished by religious flames of judgment and legalism.

Then some things happened that shockingly crushed my trust in my parents and God.

The only comfort during that difficult time was a Pentecostal preaching cassette given to me by someone. It taught me to thank and praise God for all evil things and to receive them as God's gifts, as his training and testing, and to believe this to be for my very best.

I listened to the tape over and over again, trying to thank Him for the sin that had destroyed my trust and forced me to carry a painful family secret.

God, in my eyes, was ultimately divided. The secure, joyful presence of Jesus was utterly divided in me by the image of an evil god, who always wanted to test, train and send trials "for the best" – to purify, judge and to bring constant guilt. The God of the Law, the God of the Old Testament and the way He was presented to us by our preachers, felt separate from the presence of the Holy Spirit that had helped me since I was a little girl. At the age of 15 I made my resolution; to deny God for good. I ran away from home and chose to try all the godless things I could find.

I realize today that I was raped by religion. So were my parents and their parents. ELOHIM, the Creator, the true God of Israel tried to come through to us, in spite of all the lies that we believed about Him. But we did not really know Him, neither could we discern His voice. But I tasted of his presence and that I could never forget. Even when I was drunk and drugged, I kept preaching Jesus to my friends.

Finally, the day came when that presence of the Creator was brought to me without religion and with the sweet name of Yeshua, my Jewish Savior. I got to know the Good God, the undivided God (same God in both covenants!) – that His goodness brings us to repentance, which does not mean judgment and shame but rather forgiveness, returning home and empowerment to walk His ways.

> **..But God's gracious gift is eternal life in Messiah Yeshua our Lord."**
> **— Romans 6:23b**

Little by little, the marks of spiritual rape began to heal. I got to know Yeshua, the Jewish Messiah, instead of the Christian Jesus, who was so controversial, and in whose name so many people were murdered (the Holocaust, the Spanish Inquisition, and more). Yeshua is like His Father, who is so different from that legalistic "God of the Old Testament" the way He had been taught to me. I got to know Abba, and He was not religious, neither was Yeshua. I realized that both in the Old and New Covenants it's the same ELOHIM who speaks and that His Word is Eternal. His law is called Torah which has nothing to do with legalism, but rather it means instructions from our loving Father who wants our very best.

Guilt and shame were taken away and replaced by trust and love. My old master, the all-encompassing fear, could not stay in the presence of love. It began to fade away. And it keeps on fading away all the time as I choose to believe the truth He says about Himself and about me.

The patient love of my new spiritual family brought me from death to life, and I found my place in the ministry that brought me the Messiah, without religion.

What helped me to take this amazing journey of restoration was studying Archbishop Dominiquae Bierman's GRM Israeli Video Bible School. I highly recommend it to all of you that have been raised in any form of Christianity, and that might have been wounded by religion. It will wash you clean – and you will be able to start a brand new relationship with Yeshua the Jewish Messiah, the awesome Lion from the Tribe of Judah. You will be mentored by Truth and Love and will get to know the true Father in heaven, the God of Israel. You can study online, order it home or plant it in a group form. Visit this link for more information: www.grmbibleschool.com.

I desire that you will become whole if you have been wounded by religion, and that you know that there is help for you.

—Hadassah

CHAPTER 25

THE KINGDOMS OF THIS WORLD

[Seventh Trumpet: The Kingdom Proclaimed] Then the seventh angel sounded: And there were loud voices in heaven, saying: "The kingdoms of this world have become the kingdoms of our Lord and of His Messiah, and He shall reign forever and ever!"

— *Revelation 11:15 NKJV*

On the 14th of May 2016, in the Jubilee year and the 68th Gregorian Calendar Anniversary of the establishing the miracle State of Israel, I was elevated to the position of Archbishop within TAPAC (Trans-Atlantic and Pacific Alliance of Churches) in the Holy City of Jerusalem, Israel in front of many Christian and Jewish witnesses. Archbishop is the highest position of Clerical Authority within this organization and most denominations of Christianity.

This position carries a kingly authority within the kingdom of the religious system of Christianity. This promotion makes me the first Jewish/Israeli woman Archbishop in the world and as far as I know, maybe in history. I say this for the glory of Yah (God) whom I have served throughout many tribulations and exciting moments since 1988.

Christianity, Judaism, Islam, and many others are types of "kingdoms of this world." They are not entirely the Kingdom of God. Even though they have elements that match the principles of the Kingdom of YHVH, they are still what I would call "mixed kingdoms," thus qualify to be classified as "kingdoms of this world." One day all the kingdoms of this world will be incorporated into the Kingdom of God! For that to happen, it is mandatory for their content and function to become unified with YHVH's Word and Spirit. In other words, every religious denomination, system, or empire, financial or national, and any other kingdom of this world will have to undergo a severe transformation from within. This transformation will enable them to submit and surrender to the King of kings and Adon Haadonim (LORD of lords), Yeshua the Jewish Messiah and Lion from the Tribe of Judah.

THE POWER TO INFLUENCE

Being set in a position of authority, having kingly authority within Christianity gives me the power to influence from within so that this transformation can happen and the scripture can be fulfilled. We are indeed at the end of the age, and all kingdoms will be judged. This judgment is especially true for what we call *"the House of God."*

> For the time has come for judgment to begin at the house of God; and if it begins with us first, what will be the end of those who do not obey the gospel of God?
>
> — 1 Peter 4:17

The House of God is those that consider themselves followers of the Savior that was crucified, buried and rose from the dead over 2,000 years ago in Jerusalem, Israel. His real name is Yeshua, though many still call Him by the Greek name, Jesus Christ. He was, is and will be a *Jew*; by a Jew, the world gets saved, and by a Jew, the world will be judged:

> But one of the elders said to me, "Do not weep. Behold, the Lion of the tribe of Judah, the Root of David, has prevailed to open the scroll and to loose its seven seals."
>
> — Revelation 5:5

Out of this necessary Judgment, from all the different denominations and religious kingdoms, a purified Bride will be gathered. This purified Bride will lead a dying world, by the power of the Spirit, to the source of Living Water—Yeshua Himself.

> And the Spirit and the bride say, "Come!" And let him who hears say, "Come!" And let him who thirsts come. Whoever desires, let him take the water of life freely.
>
> — Revelation 22:17

This Bride will be *unified* by the Spirit of Truth and will fulfill the prayer of Messiah in John 17 when Yeshua prayed that Jew and Gentile would become one (*echad*) so the world will believe. *Echad* is a Hebrew word, and it means "oneness in plurality," which means that this Bride will be comprised of people from every walk of life, from every kingdom and every religious system, every tongue, tribe, and nation:

> And they sang a new song, saying: "You are worthy to take the scroll, And to open its seals; For You were slain, And have redeemed us to God by Your blood Out of every tribe and tongue and people and nation.
> — Revelation 5:9

UNITY BY THE SPIRIT OF TRUTH

> And I will pray to the Father, and He will give you another Helper, that He may abide with you forever— the Spirit of truth, whom the world cannot receive, because it neither sees Him nor knows Him; but you know Him, for He dwells with you and will be in you. I will not leave you orphans; I will come to you.
> — John 14:16-18

What will unify this powerful, pure Bride will be the Spirit of Truth. She will not be united by the color of skin, by any worldly dress code or by any cultural traditions. She will be unified by the Spirit of Truth alone; she will be sanctified by the Truth of Yah's Word as interpreted by the Spirit of Truth – Ruach Haemet: And Truth is not "truths."

> Sanctify them by Your truth. Your word is truth. "I do not pray for these alone, but also for those who will believe in Me through their word; that they all may be one, as You, Father, are in Me, and I in

You; that they also may be one in Us, that the world may believe that You sent Me.

— John 17:17, 20-21

Maybe many roads lead to Rome, but only *one* way leads to the Kingdom of God:

Yeshua said to him, "I am the way, the truth, and the life. No one comes to the Father except through Me.

— John 14:6

And Yeshua being the Way, Truth and Life is a Jew. The Holy Scriptures were mostly written by Hebrews in Covenant with the Almighty through the Torah and Commandments that He gave them to share with all of mankind. So this purified Bride will stand in the truth of the Biblical Hebrew foundations, forsaking the Roman mixture that crept into the Church during the 4th Century. The Eastern Roman Emperor Constantine and the Council of Nicaea divorced her from the Jews and everything Jewish, including the very name of the Savior, Yeshua, which means "salvation!"

THE TRANSFORMATION OF THE CHRISTIAN CHURCH

Therefore, to be used by YHVH in the transformation of the Religious Kingdom of Christianity, I have obeyed Him, and after much prayer accepted the position of Archbishop. As I did so, I was given the liberty as a Jewish Archbishop, to revise the liturgy of this powerful ceremony so my vows would match my principles of faith as an End-time Messianic, Apostolic, Prophetic Apostle-Prophet. I have been received into this honorable position in the full capacity of who I am, what I believe, and what I have represented since I have obeyed the divine call to Apostolic Ministry given to me from Jerusalem and the U.K. in 1989.

> For if you remain completely silent at this time, relief and deliverance will arise for the Jews from another place, but you and your father's house will perish. Yet who knows whether you have come to the kingdom for such a time as this?"
>
> — Esther 4:14

The favor of YHVH has been upon me like it was upon Queen Esther in Persia, Prophet Daniel in Babylon, and Joseph in Egypt, who did not need to compromise their Godly faith principles to effectuate historical change in the ruling empires of their time. And for that, I am grateful and give all the glory to Yah!

MY MESSIANIC APOSTOLIC PROPHETIC VOWS

Here is a synopsis of my vows as I have proclaimed them in my Inauguration Ceremony as Archbishop of TAPAC.

The Archbishop-elect says:

I, Adriana Dominiquae Bierman, do so affirm, and accordingly declare my belief in the faith which is revealed in the Holy Scriptures and instituted by Yeshua and his Jewish Apostles. I will use only the forms of service which are authorized or allowed by the Messianic tradition as anointed by the Holy Spirit and rooted and grounded in the principles of the Holy Scriptures.

Fully understanding that the Church is in a process of restoration to the original Hebrew foundations of faith as grafted into the Olive Tree with the people of Israel. In every generation there are moves of restoration in order to restore all things as written in Acts 3:19 and I commit myself to submit, by the grace of Yah, to all His ordained moves of restoration so as to walk in the full truth of His Kingdom.

MY FIRST TEACHING AND ASSIGNMENT AS ARCHBISHOP

My first teaching after my Elevation Ceremony, during the Jerusalem Bishops Forum, was the comparison between the Pagan Feasts that have been adopted by Christianity and the original and Eternal Biblical Moadim or Holy Festivals, as depicted in Leviticus 23.

This urgency to forsake Replacement Theology altogether is necessary as the Judgment of the Church is knocking at the doors of every kingdom of this world and every religious denomination! Amid this coming Judgment, a mighty revival and the Greatest Harvest ever seen is about to break out.

I consider myself privileged and humbled to be considered worthy to serve our King, Yeshua in this manner. I hope and pray that all of you, our disciples, partners, and friends, will stand together with me in prayer and support until all the kingdoms of this world submit to our Jewish Messiah, Yeshua.

CHAPTER 26

BOLD AS A LION
EXPEL THE DARKNESS

> For behold, darkness will cover the earth and deep darkness the peoples; but YHVH will rise upon you and His glory will appear upon you. "Nations will come to your light, and kings to the brightness of your rising.
>
> — *Isaiah 60:2-3*

WHAT A TIME we are living in! These are times of prophetic fulfillment, just like in 1947 when the U.N. voted to *partition* the then called Palestine, which is the Biblical Land of Israel, into two nations – one Arab and one Jewish. The Arabs *rejected* the resolution of the U.N., and thus lost the opportunity *forever* to become a nation in the Land of Israel.

Then in 1967 in a political attempt to gain sympathy and support for their goal of taking over all of the land of Israel in order to create an Arab-only state, they changed their designation from Arabs living in Palestine, (just like there were Brits or Jews living in Palestine) to the name of "Palestinians."

They have made the world believe that a people called "Palestinians" actually exist and have existed forever. (Eretzyisroel.org)

This is a *big*, fat lie that has had all the nations in *darkness* and deep deception.

Now the 151 nations that sided with the U.N. resolution of November 30, 2017 (100 years after the Balfour Declaration on November 2, 1917) to disavow Jerusalem from the Jewish people, plus the nine nations that abstained, thereby failing to stand with the Jewish people, are deep in the Valley of Judgment of the Almighty God of Israel and have nothing to expect but *trouble* and catastrophes:

> **And in that day I will set about to destroy all the nations that come against Jerusalem.**
>
> **– Zechariah 12:9**

All that because *one* man, the Grand Muslim Mufti of Jerusalem, by the name of *Haj Amin El Husseini*—who was the most important Islamic figure during the Nazi Shoah (Holocaust) and the Second World War—concocted a hideous plan!

THE PALESTINIAN CAUSE = THE FINAL SOLUTION

Haj Amin El Husseini visited Hitler in 1941 and asked the Fuhrer to raise him an army in the land of Israel that had been renamed "Palestine" by the Roman occupiers in the 1st Century (meaning *Philistine*). What kind of Army? He requested the evilest man that ever lived to raise him an army like the Nazi Army. An army with one purpose and only one purpose, to implement the Final Solution that Hitler so loved, to annihilate *all* the Jews in Palestine, once and for all. Hitler gladly complied and trained this Arab Army as he prepared his own Nazi Army. Out of this plan, the whole "Palestinian Cause" developed. That's right, the Palestinian Cause, which includes the PLO, the Fatah, Hamas, Hezbollah and all the way to ISIS, is the "Love Child of Hitler."

Now think about this, all these 151+9 U.N. nations that have disavowed Jerusalem from the Jewish people, have *officially* and *publicly* sided with Hitler for the annihilation of Israel.

> O God, do not remain quiet; Do not be silent and, O God, do not be still. For behold, Your enemies make an uproar, And those who hate You have exalted themselves. They make shrewd plans against Your people, And conspire together against Your treasured ones. They have said, "Come, and let us wipe them out as a nation, That the name of Israel be remembered no more." For they have conspired together with one mind; Against You they make a covenant.
>
> – Psalm 83:1-5

EXPEL THE DARKNESS OF NEUTRALITY AND PASSIVITY

> Deliver those who are being taken away to death, And those who are staggering to slaughter, Oh hold them back. If you say, "See, we did not know this," Does He not consider it who weighs the hearts? And does He not know it who keeps your soul? And will He not render to man according to his work?
> — Proverbs 24:11-12

Are you a citizen in one of those nations that are included in the U.N.'s anti-Israel, anti-Jerusalem, anti-God resolution? *If so, please be warned, even if you are a believer in Messiah, and you are doing nothing about this predicament, then you will be in the "same boat" as your nation!*

And I assure you that this "boat" is going to *sink* rapidly! YHVH does not have any time to waste until He restores *all* of Israel as He has promised in numerous scriptures in the Bible. He is in a hurry to restore Zion, His dwelling place, and that means Israel with Jerusalem as its capital. In fact, the Messiah will soon return and will set His rulership on the earth in Yerushalayim, on the Temple Mount. He will not rule from a Mosque; neither shall His Holy City be called *Al Quds*. And I promise you that the chants all over the City will not be "*Allah Akbar!*" which means "Allah is the greatest." But instead, Halelu-*Yah* or "praise to Yah," who is YHVH, the God of Israel.

> On your walls, O Jerusalem, I have appointed watchmen; All day and all night they will never keep silent. You who remind the Lord, take

no rest for yourselves; And give Him no rest until He establishes and makes Jerusalem a praise in the earth.

— Isiah 62:6-7

So back to you, beloved Believer in Messiah. The God of Israel is not one to sanction neutrality or passivity or inactivity. *If you are in one of those nations that have come against Israel and Jerusalem, then you and your family and your Christian friends are in danger.* You see, the same Arabs that are now called "Palestinians" have been sanctioned by the U.N. to *annihilate* Israel! One of the nations that voted to sanction this annihilation is *Germany*. Others include *all* the European countries and Africa, most of the Pacific, South America, Asia, and the Middle East.

OVER SEVEN AND A HALF BILLION PEOPLE ARE IN DANGER OF TOTAL DESTRUCTION!

If you think that I am a sensationalist or I am exaggerating, please read below what the King of the Jews, the Creator of heaven and earth Himself says about it:

> Draw near, O nations, to hear; and listen, O peoples! Let the earth and all it contains hear, and the world and all that springs from it. For the Lord's indignation is against all the nations, And His wrath against all their armies; He has utterly destroyed them, He has given them over to slaughter. So their slain will be thrown out, And their corpses will give off their stench, and the mountains will be drenched with their blood.
>
> — Isaiah 34:1-3

Why is He bent on destroying *all* the nations? He continues in the same chapter:

> For YHVH has a day of vengeance, a year of recompense for the cause of Zion.
>
> — Isaiah 34:8

He is about to take *revenge* for all the blood of His Jewish people that has been spilled on the earth. This includes not only the recent U.N. resolutions, but also all the blood spilt in the name of Jesus Christ and Christianity through the Crusades, the Spanish and Portuguese Inquisitions, the pogroms, the untold expulsions, humiliations, the Nazi Shoah (Holocaust), to all the Anti-Zionism in the U.N., and all the Christian NGO's that have sided with the "Palestinian Cause" with their money and their voices. The entire United Nations have sided with Hitler's plan through Haj Amin El Husseini, the PLO, the Fatah and the Palestinian Cause – a Trojan horse to destroy Israel.

PASSIVITY IS THE SAME AS SIDING WITH THE ENEMY!

Yeshua will separate the nations according to how they have treated the Jewish people; not only if they did something against them, but also if they did *nothing* to help them when needed:

> Then He will also say to those on His left, 'Depart from Me, accursed ones, into the eternal fire which has been prepared for the devil and his angels; for I was hungry, and you gave Me nothing to eat; I was thirsty, and you gave Me nothing to drink;   I was a stranger, and you did not invite Me in; naked, and you did not clothe Me;

sick, and in prison, and you did not visit Me.' Then they themselves also will answer, 'Lord, when did we see You hungry, or thirsty, or a stranger, or naked, or sick, or in prison, and did not take care of You?' Then He will answer them, 'Truly I say to you, to the extent that you did not do it to one of the least of these, you did not do it to Me.' These will go away into eternal punishment, but the righteous into eternal life."

— Matthew 25:41-46

Who are the "least of these" that Yeshua is referring to? The least of the Jewish people He was speaking to.

YOU ARE YOUR NATION!

I searched for a man among them who would build up the wall and stand in the gap before Me for the land, so that I would not destroy it; but I found no one.

— Ezekiel 22:30

You will not be able to stand before Yeshua, the King of the Jews and say, "I could do nothing about it! It just happened," because He will hold each one of us accountable. Did we raise our voices to rebuke and dispel this darkness? Did we *act* for Israel's sake? Did we spend some effort *seeking him* as to what to do? Did we *support* financially, and in *serious* prayer, the cause of Zion? Or where we just like the German and Polish Christians that *smelled* the Jews being burned in the crematorium of the death camps and continued *singing* from their hymnals in the churches! They were too busy protecting themselves by *pretending* to ignore the terrible slaughter the Jews were going through. They were too steeped in the hateful

Christian Replacement Theology to care. There were only a *very few* who rose up against the Nazi regime or who *acted* to rescue Jews, and we *salute them*! But there were too few, and not *one* Christian organization stood up to Hitler, not one.

And what about now in the 21st Century with this modern-day plan to use the U.N. to exterminate Israel officially? Do you really think that you can escape because you are a Christian or even Messianic? Beloved ones, the same radical Muslims that want to exterminate every Jew, want to eradicate you too! They are bent on Islam ruling the world, not Judaism or Christianity, only Islam.

WE ARE NOT OUT OF HARM'S WAY BELOVEDS!

But really, the *one* we should fear the most is the God of Israel Himself, not radical Islam. He promised to destroy the nations that have come against Jerusalem. And that includes *your* nation! Unless...

YOU RISE UP LIKE THE ANCIENT MACCABEES TO EXPEL THE DARKNESS; LIGHTING UP YOUR NATION'S HANUKKAH MENORAH!

> Arise, shine; for your light has come, and the glory of YHVH has risen upon you.
>
> — Isaiah 60:1

The Maccabees were Jewish priests who stood up against the mighty Greek Empire that was bent on conquering all of Israel and forcing the Jewish people into idolatry. They had overtaken the Holy Temple on the Temple Mount and were burning pigs on the altar. Then this small band of Jewish priests arose and defied them all! They took the Temple back and cleansed it from all idolatry. By faith in the miracles of YHVH, the God of Israel they re-instituted Divine Worship and relit the Seven Branch Menorah. Thus, they expelled the darkness of their time!

They did this at a high cost, against all the odds, risking their lives at every turn. Doing what was *right* in the eyes of YHVH was much more dear to them than preserving their lives.

> But I have this against you, that you have left your first love. Therefore remember from where you have fallen, and repent and do the deeds you did at first; or else I am coming to you and will remove your lampstand (Menorah!) out of its place— unless you repent.
> — Revelation 2:4.5

ARE YOU LIKE NOAH OR AS THE REST THAT DROWNED?

> And just as it happened in the days of Noah, so it will be also in the days of the Son of Man: they were eating, they were drinking, they were marrying, they were being given in marriage, until the day that Noah entered the ark, and the flood came and destroyed them all.
> — Luke 17:26-27

Noah was building an Ark because ELOHIM-God (the God of Israel) was about to destroy the world because of their wickedness and rebellion. But He had given instructions to *one* man on how to build a *boat* big enough to rescue as many people and as many animals as possible. However, besides his own family, *no one* else wanted to help him in the project.

They mocked him, and did not believe that it would rain, as it had never rained like that before. They did not believe in the warnings of righteous Noah that ELOHIM-the Creator was about to eradicate *all* of humanity. *When the flood came, they all perished because of unbelief in the Judgment of God! I am sure there were some religious people among them, but they had no Fear of Yah (God).*

A *false gospel* has been preached in the 21st Century whereabouts God is too *good* to judge or to destroy. Do not believe it for a moment. The God of the New Testament is *precisely* the same one as in the "Old" Testament (the Holy Scriptures), and the same principles apply today as applied in the Days of Noah!

ALL THE MACCABEES ARE CALLED TO COME ON-BOARD!

During this fateful, historical time of all the world (minus five countries) turning against Israel, Jerusalem and the Jewish people, we are building Noah's Ark again: It is called the *United Nations For Israel*.

We invite you to *board the ark* and *act* with us during these dangerous times to *support* Israel actively, to *stand* with her like Ruth with Naomi, and to turn *your* nation from a prominent Goat Nation into a Sheep Nation, *one person at a time.*

ARE YOU A SON OF ZION OR A SON OF GREECE?

For I will bend Judah as My bow, I will fill the bow with Ephraim. And I will stir up your sons, O Zion, against your sons, O Greece; And I will make you like a warrior's sword. Then YHVH will appear over them, and His arrow will go forth like lightning; and YHVH God will blow the trumpet, (Shofar!)

— Zechariah 9:13-14

Either you are a modern-day Maccabee—a Son or Daughter of Zion and stand up against unrighteousness—or you are a son or daughter of Greece, a "Greek Idolater" (steeped in Replacement Theology, Romanized Christianity, pagan feasts and lukewarm or prideful towards Israel). *Either you board the United Nations for Israel or you stand with the present-day U.N. against Israel. Neutrality is not acceptable in eyes of YHVH.*

This is not a church, neither just a ministry: This is a movement just like the Maccabees of old and like the building of Noah's Ark.

Let us work while it is still day, as the night is coming. Expel the deception of darkness: Spirits of Replacement Theology; Anti-messiah; Anti-Israel; Anti-Torah; Anti-Jewish; and Anti-Zionist's *now* from your life, your family, church, ministry and as many people as possible. Tomorrow may be too late!

We welcome the modern-day Maccabees and Noah-like people to help us build the Ark called the United Nations for Israel, transforming *your* nation into a Sheep Nation, one person at a time.

Everyone on-board? The doors are about to close! It is YHVH Himself that shut the doors of Noah's Ark, and it is He that will do it again. How long do we have until the time is up?

We must work the works of Him who sent Me as long as it is day; night is coming when no one can work.

— John 9:4

CHAPTER 27

MY QUEEN ESTHER

> Then Queen Esther, daughter of Abihail, with Mordecai the Jew, wrote with full authority to confirm this second letter about Purim.
>
> — *Esther 9:29*

For this *Purim*, I want to bless you with my view of Queen Esther, the Jewish Hadassah. So often we read Bible stories, but we miss the human and "down to earth" part, and we only see the heroic. However, the heroic is actually a result of the humanity of the hero (or heroine) in our case. Let us meet my Queen Esther:

> He was bringing up Hadassah, that is Esther, his uncle's daughter, for she had no father or mother. Now the young lady was beautiful of form and face, and when her father and her mother died, Mordecai took her as his own daughter.
>
> — *Esther 2:7*

First off, Esther is a young woman; maybe 16 or 17 years old. She is a virgin, one who has never known a man intimately. As all teenagers do, she may have had dreams of the "knight in shining armor" she would one day fall in love with and marry. Surely the King of Persia was not one of her prospects! As sheltered as she grew under the tutelage of her uncle Mordecai, she was an orphan with a capital "o." She had no mother, no father, no sisters and no brothers that we know of. She may have never met her parents, or maybe she was very young when they died. Being an exile and a captive from Judah it may very well be that her parents were murdered by the Persian authorities, maybe by the King himself, or perhaps they died when Jerusalem fell into the hands of Babylon before Persia took over the Empire.

The Bible is silent about the circumstances of their death, but one thing we know is that it is not happy to be an orphan. It is not happy for a little girl to lack a mother to caress her, to comfort her in a foreign land. Even though Mordecai became an excellent surrogate father it seems while growing up and becoming a woman (getting her period and such things that happen to young maidens) she had no mother to confide in. Maybe she grew up lonely, serving her uncle the best she could, but it seems to me that Hadassah's beginnings were not very favorable – indeed, she did not have the marks of distinction to royalty or happy life.

It looks to me that though Hadassah had suffered from a very young age, she had made a few personal choices that are Royal in my eyes. Her choices included: First, to fear the God of her fathers (the God of Israel). Second, to honor her adopted father, Uncle Mordecai. Third, to have a positive, humble attitude in life. This non-victim attitude is what brought Hadassah to the throne and positioned her to become the savior of her people Israel. We can see evidence of that positive, faith attitude when she was kidnapped from the safety of Uncle Mordecai's home into the harem of the King.

> **So it came about when the command and decree of the king were heard and many young ladies were gathered to the citadel of Susa into the custody of Hegai, that Esther was taken to the king's palace into the custody of Hegai, who was in charge of the women.**
>
> **— Esther 2:8**

Talk about a traumatic event! Imagine all the girls screaming in sheer terror as they were being seized by the Persian soldiers to be taken to a women's luxury jail called a Harem, from where they would *never* be able to return to their homes and their families. Their life was doomed to seclusion. And even if the king would choose one of them, things would not be much better. The chosen lady would have to make love to the king whether she liked him or not; none of her feelings would be taken into consideration. Her goal in life would be to please the king whenever he wanted her and live in seclusion among the other women-concubines and the eunuchs in the luxury of the harem. The day these girls were seized as "merchandise" was the day their dreams died. Plus consider that only one will be chosen and all the others would be nothing but an ornament, a toy with no aspirations for a family of their own. The king may call on each of his concubines at times, but that was the most they could hope for and maybe if they were "lucky" they would fall pregnant and raise a royal child of their own.

> **Esther had not revealed her people or family, for Mordecai had charged her not to reveal it.**
>
> — Esther 2:10

It is no surprise therefore that, when the time came for each of these women to go to the king and see if they would be chosen – after months of preparation and grooming in precious oils, each one decided the best they could wear to impress the king. There was quite a women's competition going on in that harem. Once their initial first shock of captivity subsided, each woman was then totally focused on conquering the heart of the king and to reach the crown. Except Hadassah, who that by then had adopted the pagan name, Esther.

Esther is a derivative from *Ishtar* (the goddess of fertility), but it also has a Hebrew meaning, "the hidden one." And indeed she was hiding her identity as a Jew, as Uncle Mordecai had wisely advised, under her pagan name. Esther kept obeying her uncle, though far away from him. This decision shows me that she had a pliable, teachable heart of obedience but it also shows courage. Courage to act a part in a role that she had not planned on and she had not scripted, and courage to trust her uncle's wisdom, her upbringing as a Yah-fearing Jew of her fathers God.

> Now when the turn of Esther, the daughter of Abihail the uncle of Mordecai who had taken her as his daughter, came to go in to the king, she did not request anything except what Hegai, the king's eunuch who was in charge of the women, advised. And Esther found favor in the eyes of all who saw her.
>
> — Esther 2:15

Esther was the only one that relinquished her "rights" in the harem. She deferred her rights of choice of garments for her defining night with the king to the eunuch in charge. The obedience, humility, and teachability that she had displayed in her uncle's home brought her favor with the eunuchs in authority. She was different, and she was not playing the part of a seductress like the others. She simply wanted the advice of professionals and, when it came to the king, the eunuch knew exactly what his master liked the most. He proceeded to dress her up in a way that would be irresistible to the king. Her discrete demeanor, her humble spirit, her positive and wise attitude now was "packaged" in the right "wrapping," dressed in the clothes and jewelry the king liked best.

I wonder *what exactly did these clothes look like? Were they concealing or revealing? Were they shiny and glitzy or toned down in color? Were the earrings long or round, gold or silver, jade or diamonds?* Again, the Scriptures are silent about the details which allow our imaginations to soar. One thing does cross my mind: I am sure that her garments did not look "Jewish." Probably in the eyes of most Jews she would have looked like a "pagan and unholy woman" going to the King. Maybe had they been able to see her they would have disapproved of her make-up, her cape, her dress, her gown and the Persian symbols in them. But this is what the eunuch advised, and he knew the king best.

> **The king loved Esther more than all the women, and she found favor and kindness with him more than all the virgins, so that he set the royal crown on her head and made her queen instead of Vashti.**
>
> **– Esther 2:17**

I cannot refrain from thinking about my own life: When I have had to dress in Bishop's and Archbishop's clothes (that do not look Jewish but rather Catholic), and yet this is what my "eunuch," the Ruach HaKodesh, the Holy Spirit requires of me – in order to play my part for the salvation of many. I admire Queen Esther for not allowing religiosity or the fear of man to stop her divine mission of which she knew nothing at that time. She was just following instructions. And indeed, the king was pleased! Pleased with her outer garments and satisfied with her beauty and character. It was love at first sight for him. The question is what *was it for her*? Did she like him? Was he attractive? Was he gentle? After all, this would be the only man she would ever know.

> **Esther had not yet made known her kindred or her people, even as Mordecai had commanded her; for Esther did what Mordecai told her as she had done when under his care.**
>
> **– Esther 2:20**

As I continue sharing my Queen Esther with you, I want to touch on her human tendency to comply. While I praise her teachability and submissiveness that won her so much favor with the authorities and with the king himself, there is an area of compliance in her character that was not to her advantage. That is the reason why perhaps the king grew bored with her, and for one month he did not reach out to her. She had become a forgotten queen. Maybe she was too compliant, too sweet and the king needed someone more exciting. It looks to me that this passivity led her to accept the situation instead of fighting back for the affections of the king. She grew comfortable in her passivity and settled for less than she could have, less than she could be – sitting in the luxury and comfort of the harem among other women that were in the same predicament. I can even detect a hint of depression here, maybe discouragement?

> **When Mordecai learned all that had been done, he tore his clothes, put on sackcloth and ashes, and went out into the midst of the city and wailed loudly and bitterly.**
>
> **– Esther 4:1**

Suddenly her lonely, comfortable, sleepy world of comfort and royal entertainment was rocked by the news. Her beloved and honored uncle Mordecai was fighting a decree of extermination signed by the king! He was in dust and ashes as soon as he learned that the wicked counselor of the king, Haman the Agagite (a descendant of Amalek, the feared enemy of Israel) had convinced the king to exterminate all the Jews! Alas! It was a day of distress and destruction, and there was no salvation in sight: Whatever was signed by the King's signet ring could not be revoked.

> Then Esther spoke to Hathach and ordered him to reply to Mordecai: "All the king's servants and the people of the king's provinces know that for any man or woman who comes to the king to the inner court who is not summoned, he has but one law, that he be put to death, unless the king holds out to him the golden scepter so that he may live. And I have not been summoned to come to the king for these thirty days.
>
> — Esther 4:10-11

However, the compliant Esther was not moved to come out of her passivity. She had found her comfort zone and did not want to suffer anymore. Had she not suffered enough already as a Jewish captive, an exile, an orphan, a kidnapped woman and now rejected by the king that had not seen her in 30 days? Do I detect a hint of "victim mentality" here? Do I detect some bitterness in her attitude, maybe resentment? There is a time in the life of all heroes and heroines where "too much is too much" and when we feel we cannot give any more of ourselves. This is a human moment in the life of a hero, an important moment. It is a moment of definition. Choices made at this point will define all future events. Will Queen Esther rise as a queen or will she remain a captive, an exiled orphan? Her positive attitudes and choices made her a queen, and now?

> Then Mordecai told them to reply to Esther, "Do not imagine that you in the king's palace can escape any more than all the Jews. For

> if you remain silent at this time, relief and deliverance will arise for the Jews from another place and you and your father's house will perish. And who knows whether you have not attained royalty for such a time as this?"
>
> — Esther 4:13-14

Mordecai knew how to speak to the heart of his treasured niece; after all, he had raised her. He knew her better than herself, knowing what would propel her forward and get her out of her shell to take bold *action*! He rebuked her as only he could. He talked to "his Hadassah," the courageous Jewish woman: He spoke to her faith and conscience, and she responded as Jewish Hadassah would. She had been Esther-*Ishtar*-hidden for too long – she needed to show up in her Jewishness now or never.

> Then Esther told them to reply to Mordecai, "Go, assemble all the Jews who are found in Susa, and fast for me; do not eat or drink for three days, night or day. I and my maidens also will fast in the same way. And thus I will go in to the king, which is not according to the law; and if I perish, I perish."
>
> — Esther 4:15-16

Putting all fear aside, as this was an actual matter of life and death, she mustered all the courage she could. She exercised leadership and authority as she commanded all the Jews and all her handmaidens to fast with her.

> So it was, when the king saw Queen Esther standing in the court, that she found favor in his sight, and the king held out to Esther

the golden scepter that was in his hand. Then Esther went near and touched the top of the scepter.

— Esther 5:2

She was a strategic thinker: She had a plan, and no one would stop her. Hadassah and Esther had become *one* finally! Her Jewishness and her faith, coupled with her position of authority and royalty, would now manage to perform the greatest feat any man or woman had ever achieved. She would rescue the entire Jewish Nation from extermination and would become a Queen for real – sitting side by side with the King on her throne. She would rise from the obscurity of the harem into the limelight and responsibility of the Throne. Still dressed in Royal, Persian garments, full of the Spirit of Israel and of Israel's God she would co-rule Persia – and her Uncle would become the advisor of the king instead of the wicked Amalekite Haman. She single-handedly defeated the Principality of Amalek and rescued Israel from extinction!

Had it not been for Queen Esther, the Messiah Yeshua would not have been born of the Tribe of Judah and the House of David, prophecy would not have been fulfilled, and no Gentiles would ever be able to enjoy salvation and redemption! Had it not been for the overcoming courage and obedience of one Jewish woman, the whole world would now be doomed to destruction. The devil has tried to annihilate Israel so that the nations would never experience salvation. He is still trying to destroy Israel so that the Messiah will not return to Jerusalem.

So King Ahasuerus said to Queen Esther and to Mordecai the Jew, "Behold, I have given the house of Haman to Esther, and him they have hanged on the gallows because he had stretched out his hands against the Jews."

— Esther 8:7

"All hail Queen Esther!" You are still needed in this generation!

For such a time as this.

— Esther 4:14

APPENDIX I

GET EQUIPPED & PARTNER WITH US

GLOBAL REVIVAL MAP (GRM) ISRAELI BIBLE SCHOOL

Take the most comprehensive video Bible school online that focuses on dismantling replacement theology.
For more information or to order, please contact us:
www.grmbibleschool.com
grm@dominiquaebierman.com

UNITED NATIONS FOR ISRAEL MOVEMENT

We invite you to join us as a member and partner with $25 a month, which supports the advancing of this End time vision that will bring true unity to the body of the Messiah. We will see the One New Man form, witness the restoration of Israel, and take part in the birthing of *Sheep Nations*. Today is an exciting time to be serving Him!
www.unitednationsforisrael.org
info@unitednationsforisrael.org

GLOBAL RE-EDUCATION INITIATIVE (GRI) AGAINST ANTI-SEMITISM

Discover the Jewishness of Jesus and defeat Christian anti-Semitism with this online video course to see revival in your nation!
www.against-antisemitism.com
info@against-antisemitism.com

JOIN OUR ANNUAL ISRAEL TOURS

Travel through the Holy Land and watch the Hebrew Holy Scriptures come alive.
www.kad-esh.org/tours-and-events/

TO SEND OFFERINGS TO SUPPORT OUR WORK

Your help keeps this mission of restoration going far and wide.
www.kad-esh.org/donations

CONTACT US

Archbishop Dr. Dominiquae & Rabbi Baruch Bierman
Kad-Esh MAP Ministries | www.kad-esh.org
info@kad-esh.org
United Nations for Israel | www.unitednationsforisrael.org
info@unitednationsforisrael.org
Zion's Gospel Press | shalom@zionsgospel.com
52 Tuscan Way, Ste 202-412, 32092,
St. Augustine Florida, USA
+1-972-301-7087

APPENDIX II
BIBLIOGRAPHY

Demonbuster.com. "Demonbuster - Martial Arts, Yoga and Eastern Religions." *Demonbuster.com*, 2020, www.demonbuster.com/martial1.html. Accessed 9 Dec. 2020.

Amazing Discoveries. "The Pagan Origins of Mass | Catholic Church Teachings." *Amazingdiscoveries.Org*, 2009, amazingdiscoveries.org/S-deception_paganism_Catholic_mass_silver.

Barnavi, Eli. "Kabbalah: Origins of a Spiritual Adventure." My Jewish Learning, *My Jewish Learning*, 25 June 2003, www.myjewishlearning.com/article/kabbalah-origins-of-a-spiritual-adventure/. Accessed 9 Dec. 2020.

Barnett, James Harwood (1984). *The American Christmas: A Study in National Culture.* Ayer Publishing. p. 3. ISBN 0-405-07671-1.

Bevere, John. The Bait of Satan. Lake Mary, FL: Charisma House, 2014. Print.

Blessedquietness.com. "Evergreens and the Christmas Tree

Origins, Traditions." *Blessedquietness.com*, 2020, www.blessedquietness.com/journal/resource/xmastr2.htm. Accessed 9 Dec. 2020.

Carm.org. "The Origins and History of Kabbalah | CARM.org." *Carm.org*, 5 Dec. 2008, carm.org/origins-and-history-kabbalah. Accessed 9 Dec. 2020.

Casper, Jayson. "Spanning the Great Schism Between Evangelical and Orthodox Christians." *ChristianityToday.Com*, Christianity Today, 18 May 2018, www.christianitytoday.com/ct/2018/june/spanning-great-schism-eastern-othodoxy-evangelicals-unity.html.

Chabad.org. "The 7 Noahide Laws: Universal Morality." @ *chabad*, 31 Oct. 2002, www.chabad.org/library/article_cdo/aid/62221/jewish/The-7-Noahide-Laws-Universal-Morality.htm. Accessed 9 Dec. 2020.

Eretzyisroel.org. "The History of the Words Palestine And Palestinians." *Eretzyisroel.org*, 2020, www.eretzyisroel.org/~jkatz/meaning.html. Accessed 9 Dec. 2020.

Feuerstein, Georg (2012). *The Yoga Tradition: Its History, Literature, Philosophy and Practice*. Hohm Press. ISBN 978-1-935387-39-8.

Fordham.edu. "Internet History Sourcebooks Project." *Fordham.Edu*, 2020, sourcebooks.fordham.edu/source/const1-easter.asp. Accessed 9 Dec. 2020.

History.com Editors. "History of Christmas Trees." *HISTORY*, 12 Sept. 2018, www.history.com/topics/christmas/history-of-christmas-trees. Accessed 3 Sept. 2019.

Kabbalah.info. "Kabbalah Sources." *Kabbalah.Info*, 2020, www.kabbalah.info/engkab/what_is_kabbalah/what_does_kabbalah_teach.htm#.XXDQ4ChKguU. Accessed 9 Dec. 2020.

malariasite.com. "Efforts of Malaria Control." *Malaria Site*, malariasite.com, 25 Feb. 2015, www.malariasite.com/history-control/. Accessed 8 Dec. 2020.

Marling, Karal Ann (2000). *Merry Christmas!: Celebrating America's Greatest Holiday*. Harvard University Press. p. 44. ISBN 0-674-00318-7.

Medlineplus.gov. "How Can Gene Mutations Affect Health and Development?: MedlinePlus Genetics." *Medlineplus.Gov*, 2020, medlineplus.gov/genetics/understanding/mutationsanddisorders/mutationscausedisease/. Accessed 9 Dec. 2020.

Melina, Remy. "The Surprising Truth: Christians Once Banned Christmas." *Livescience.Com*, Live Science, 14 Dec. 2010, www.livescience.com/32891-why-was-christmas-banned-in-america-.html

Nazarenesoftheworld.info. "The Shocking Pagan Origin of Christmas! – Nazarene Notes." *Nazarenesoftheworld.Info*, 2020, nazarenesoftheworld.info/pagan-holidays/shocking-pagan-origin-christmas/. Accessed 9 Dec. 2020.

Oxford University Press. "yoga, n." *OED Online*. Oxford University Press. September 2015. Retrieved 9 September 2015.

Pappas, Stephanie. "Pagan Roots? 5 Surprising Facts About Christmas." *Livescience.Com*, Live Science, 23 Dec. 2012, www.livescience.com/25779-christmas-traditions-history-paganism.html.

Percival, Dr. Henry. *"The Nicean and post Nicean Fathers."* Vol. XIV Grand Rapid: Erdmans pub. 1979, pgs. 54-55

Reversespins.com. "Guru Yoga." *Reversespins.com*, 2020, www.reversespins.com/guruyoga.html. Accessed 9 Dec. 2020.

TIME.com. "Top 10 Things You Didn't Know About Christmas - TIME." *TIME.com*, 16 Dec. 2011, content.time.com/time/specials/packages/article/0,28804,1868506_1868508_1868541,00.html. Accessed 9 Dec. 2020.

Whychristmas.com. "Why Is Christmas Celebrated on the 25th December?" *Whychristmas.com*, 2020, www.whychristmas.com/customs/25th.shtml. Accessed 9 Dec. 2020.

www.ingramcontent.com/pod-product-compliance
Lightning Source LLC
Chambersburg PA
CBHW021422070526
44577CB00001B/22